LIVING MAKES YOU
RUN LONGER

To Scott and Liam
with best wishes
Martin Bulger.

Martin Bulger has spent his working life as a schoolteacher in Seaford, East Sussex and although for many years he played club football, cricket and volleyball, it is his love of running, which began while a youngster at primary school, that has lasted and led him to run his first marathon in 1978.

Now, after 140 marathons, 7 ultras (that's events that are longer than 26.2 miles) and 1000 other shorter distance races, he can reflect on a wealth of running experiences that have enriched his life.

He cites the amazing camaraderie that exists in the running world as one of the main reasons for his continued involvement in the sport... that, and the thrill of running on the South Downs on any day in the year. A significant milestone in his commitment to running happened in 1986 when, along with friends Pete Forster and Nigel Collins, he decided to establish the Seaford Striders Running Club.

His sporting heroes are Ron Hill because of his matchless dedication to running for over half a century and Ian Botham for his all-round cricketing skills and 5-star entertainment, not forgetting his mammoth walking feats in aid of charity. After three decades of running marathons, which include winning 7 of them, occasions when he started right at the front and other times when he began as a back marker in marathons that have been hilly, flat, hot (above 100 F), cold (through snowdrifts), in torrential rain, fast, slow, overseas and underwater!!... he really should have enough experience to write a book of advice about running marathons but he condenses it all down to one sentence – "enjoy the journey as well as the arrival."

LIVING MAKES YOU
RUN LONGER

Martin Bulger

LIVING MAKES YOU RUN LONGER

Olympia Publishers
London

www.olympiapublishers.com
OLYMPIA PAPERBACK EDITION

A CIP catalogue record for this title is
available from the British Library.

ISBN: 978-1-905513-51-2

First Published in 2008

Olympia Publishers
60 Cannon Street
London
EC4N 6NP
Printed in Great Britain

Acknowledgements

I would like to offer my grateful thanks to the following athletes who have willingly shared their marathon experiences with compelling frankness and detail.

Julia Armstrong
David Beattie
Karen Bowler
Jenny Cobby
Philip Dray
John Errey
John Gill
Hugh Graham
Peter Graham
Eric Hardwick
Richard Honeyman
Peter Hooper
Linda Jennings
Lorraine Kelly
John Leather

Michael Martin
Kay McDonald
John McFarlane
Jenny Mills
Roger Ockenden
Alex Parsons
Debbie Pentland
Joyce Smith
Peter Taylor
Richard & Jacqui Walker
Bob & Jane Webster
Amanda Wilkins
Brian Winn
Bill Young
Glynis Young

Dedication

To Shirley, Graham, David and Claire Bulger who have supported my love of running with grace and enthusiasm.

And to Seaford Striders Running Club for their friendship and encouragement.

And the multitude of runners/joggers who have played their part in creating a depth of camaraderie that is the backbone of our sport.

Contents

Introduction – The Warm-up..17

The Author's Ramblings 21

Marathon Reviews...42

Contributors' Own Stories 61

The Lighter Side..98

A Short Story..111

Running Holidays & Ultra Marathons 120

Contributors' Own Stories 137

Another Short Story 175

385 yards 182

Chapter 1

Introduction – The Warm-up

If the world was going to end in two hours time, what would you do? Would you put on your running kit and trainers and go for a very long 3-hour run, probably over a favourite route? Because that's what I'd do. Please don't think that I'm fanatical or a few feathers short of a chicken. It's just that I love running and believe it to be the most natural of sporting activities and pastimes. Our muscle and bone structure has evolved to enable us to run, and run all day. So running is quite simply in our blood and for those of us who run marathons or longer distances, I suggest that we are only responding to our natural heritage, an instinct founded on survival.

If one of every species of animal on earth (including man) lined up in a race, the cheetah would be in the lead at the 100-metre point. After one mile, it would probably be the horse (but it would require a human to keep it focused). The longer the race continued, the fewer animals would be left running and soon the human representative would be the sole competitor. It is quite well known that there are still African tribes who can hunt down a deer by pursuing it relentlessly all day until it collapses exhausted.

As we don't need to catch our next meal to survive, or run fast to avoid being the next meal of some huge carnivore, why do we run? Is it really just in response to something instinctive, something deep within our being, and something that the popularity of marathons over recent decades just happens to have accidentally tapped into? It has been suggested many times that running a marathon is the ultimate athletic challenge. It certainly isn't, yet however one perceives it, the reasons why so many people tackle a marathon over and over again are much harder to explain. There are those who thrive on a challenge, people who might go white-water rafting, climb Mount Kilimanjaro before lunch, bungee jump in the buff or go scuba diving under arctic ice floes. They'll probably run a marathon as just another thrill to collect. Some may complete a marathon against all the odds, as a solitary thrust to raise funds for a charity or just to say that they've done one. They aren't thrill junkies but just ordinary people who have grabbed at a chance to 'have their day', to step outside the box and to claim their 300 minutes of fame, then return to the safe security of a 'normal' life. This book endeavours to explore the reasons why people run, what it was that persuaded them to start running and why, in particular, they run marathons. Contributions from a wide variety of marathon runners who have between them amassed about 1400 marathons, tell their own stories and offer too, marathon reviews, anecdotes and poems, to help the book uncover the mystique and passion that surrounds marathon running.

Are you one of those, for instance, who comes home from work feeling frazzled, stressed up to your eyeballs, mentally and physically exhausted and barely able to open the front door, yet moments later you are kitted out and jogging down the drive? You have metamorphosed from a dull, lifeless larva into a liberated butterfly in search of the nectar of life, (and you'll find it). You return perhaps an hour later with a sense of peace and quiet fulfilment, having wiped clean your cluttered cerebral blackboard, leaving you with the sort of feel-good factor that would make you a millionaire if you could bottle it and sell it.

So many people who I have talked with about why they started running cannot recall any particular reason and often, with a shrug of their shoulders, dismiss it as an idea that came out of the blue. Another frequent reply is "I watched the London Marathon on TV and just decided to have a go myself" – a response that's easy to understand. After more than twenty-five years it is still compulsive TV viewing and perhaps now is even more inspiring because there are fewer useless aerial shots and more close-up images. All they've got to do now is to cut down on the amount of time showing the frontrunners and devote more to the 30,000 others. This, I am certain, would appeal to even more viewers and attract greater numbers to our sport.

The amount of television coverage of marathons nowadays is proof, if it were really needed, of their popularity yet the success of the sport has developed against a backdrop of human decline and stunted endeavour. Our sad 'short cut' society is one that too often demands instant gratification, a quick fix, and invariably prefers the soft option. The dumbing down of every aspect of modern life is the accepted regime, with physical ineptitude and laziness even seen by some as praiseworthy. Is it simply a question of the more that is done for mankind the less it needs to do; a culture that is heightened by our over-reliance upon modern transport that diminishes or even removes the need to get anywhere under our own steam? And it doesn't stop there. Such things as escalators, TV remote controls and electric toothbrushes eliminate even the smallest of human actions, yet by reducing the range of simple bodily movements it also reduces the alertness and fitness of the brain impulses that generate them, and ultimately the capacity of the brain to transmit other messages that allow the body to function properly.

So many people miss out by wanting to 'arrive' without having to make the journey to get there but marathon runners are different in that they are bucking this trend of human deterioration. We are not the cranks that so many people see us as. For millions of marathon runners worldwide to be enjoying their sport and new recruits and converts joining in all the time, the question of why we run marathons becomes even more intriguing.

I'm sure that I am not the only one who has noticed an increasing number of young children who seem to have limited mobility and I don't mean just the obese and overweight youngsters. There are many who appear to lack the lithe suppleness that one associates with youthfulness. Could it be due to them having been raised on body-numbing passive entertainment such as televisions, computers and certain electronic toys instead of being allowed to grow and develop naturally?

Marathons are already dominated by older runners, so will the heat of the modern way of life dry up the pool of potential marathon runners in the years to come and threaten the future of our sport, returning it to its status of fifty years ago as something that attracts only a quirky, extreme minority? For the moment however, people of all ages and abilities are discovering running and experiencing its enormous life-changing benefits. A significant number of runners are then drawn into marathons for a variety of reasons but as to why they subsequently become hooked on the distance, it may be because of something as simple as the very act of running itself or as deep and complex as the human mind.

Chapter 2

The Author's Ramblings

It was only a few years ago, while out running on the South Downs in Sussex, between Eastbourne and Brighton, that I remembered an incident from when I was about eight years old.

I was a pupil at Hordle C of E Primary School on the southern edge of the New Forest in Hampshire, and it was playtime. It's impossible to tell what it was that influenced the games children played on the playground in the 1950s. One week, for no apparent reason, marbles would appear, have their moment of popularity, and disappear just as mysteriously. Skipping ropes, yo-yos, hoops and conkers were other crazes that would also pass in and out of favour. However, that moment of recall when running on the Downs was of the time when someone said, "let's have races across the playground."

For two energetic days boys, challenged boys, girls challenged girls, and boys occasionally challenged girls. One on one or in groups, the running craze was enjoyed by all, but what I failed to understand at the time was why I couldn't beat anyone. I loved PT lessons but I just couldn't run fast enough to beat anyone. I remember even asking a boy who was quiet, flat-footed and hated PT. He beat me too.

On the third day the same boy who had started the whole thing then suggested that instead we should run round the playground as many times as we could before our teacher, Miss Wylie, rang the bell for us to go back into class. After a few laps, most had become puffed out and stopped. I ran non-stop for the whole playtime and when the bell was rung I was the only one still running.

What I didn't realise all those years ago was that it was perhaps the first indication of my enthusiasm and capacity for long-distance running.

Not until five years later, at my senior school, when cross-country running became an alternative to the usual games lessons, i.e. the football pitch was either too waterlogged or snowbound to be played on, did I begin to realise the thrill of running. Then, during the summer term, it was the mile on the track that held my interest in running, but with a built-in safety device (a lazy streak) and no proper training the best I managed to run was 4 minutes 50 seconds before I left school for college. On reflection, for someone who was average at most things at school, running was probably what I was most successful at and even now I wonder what I could have achieved with the sort of coaching that is available nowadays.

Three years at a College of Education inevitably led to a change in lifestyle. Increased academic demands and a fuller social life shoved sport, particularly running, to the back of my mind and it wasn't until I had been teaching for five years that on one dull and boring weekend I suddenly decided to go for a run.

I was living in Seaford, a small quiet town on the East Sussex south coast and at the easterly end of the seafront was Seaford Head, a tall chalk headland, only slightly smaller than the well-known Beachy Head. Wearing a T-shirt, jeans and... plimsolls, and in a southwesterly gale, I ran the length of the seafront and up the steep path to the top of Seaford Head and back. Even now I do not know what made me do it but it did get me thinking about running again. It was late August and I decided to form a cross-country club at my school when the autumn term began.

By October the club had become a thriving nucleus of nine children aged 14 to 17. Our weekly runs increased to two after-school sessions and on each occasion we found ourselves wanting to run further and further until someone made the life-changing comment, "why don't we run a marathon?"

The conversation dried up for a few minutes while we all tried to absorb what had been said but by the time we had returned to school, we had not only made the decision to run one but had also worked out a provisional course and a likely date.

We checked the route, measured the distance with a surveyor's wheel, a bicycle milometer and an OS map to ensure it was as accurate as possible, then with the support of the school's PTA we achieved our ambition. In July 1978, long before the London Marathon captured the imagination of the British public, nine school children and their 28-year-old woodwork teacher ran a marathon. On that auspicious day, however, I had to be content with second place, 13 minutes behind one of my pupils, Stephen Knight, who cruised round in exactly 3 hours.

I had planned the route so that it returned to the school playing field at the 20-mile point, knowing that they could all achieve at least that distance. The last 6.2 miles was done around the school track so that if any runner had to pull out, it would be in the safety of the school grounds. With hindsight, this may not have been such a good idea, after all, who wants to do 24 mindless laps of a grass track in the final stages of a marathon?

An interesting recollection of our training runs was when I asked John Trenfield, one of my sixth-formers, what he thought about while on a long run. After a few moments he replied, "I have a 2000-word essay to write tonight for my A-level English. I'll think about it while running then when I get home, I'll shower, have something to eat then write out the essay, word for word, without any preparation." This is a good example of one of the mental benefits of distance running, the ability to focus, to have crystal-clear thoughts, unencumbered by the everyday junk that pollutes our brains.

That first marathon was followed by nothing more than the occasional run until early 1982 when I came across an advert for the **Robin Hood Marathon**. Those three words stung me back into action with the thought of running through Sherwood Forest, overtaking Friar Tuck, tripping up that nasty Sheriff of Nottingham and jogging alongside Maid Marion, a bizarre and pathetic notion, I agree, but it did get me running regularly again. Once I had completed it and experienced the overwhelming feeling of exhilaration again, it opened the floodgates to an interest in marathon running that has not diminished since.

On the day that I completed my hundredth marathon, which also happened to be my fiftieth birthday, a local newspaper reporter, Amanda Wilkins, presented me with a special award. Part of the wording on that award explained that in running one hundred marathons I had run 2620 miles. My quick response at the time was to liken that to running from my East Sussex home to Egypt. Thinking about it further I realised that had I been a 100-metre sprinter and completed 100 sprint races the grand total would have been a mere 10 km. In other words, from my home to Friston Church, a run that normally takes me about 40 minutes.

I have entered races of every distance from 100 metres to ultra marathons and have found each exciting and demanding in its own particular way. However, to me, the marathon is special and different from all other distances, and I don't really know why. I could point to the camaraderie of athletes thrown together by circumstance, creating a bond that helps, cajoles, sometimes rescues and frequently inspires. Or perhaps it's the picturesque scenery we often run through that paints indelible, beautiful landscapes in our memories. Maybe it's the physical and mental challenge of the marathon that combine to make it a 'whole body' experience and therefore something where absolutely no part of you can be a passive spectator. What about value for money, greed, escapism, a medal fetish? ...not me, I'm normal! A sense of achievement perhaps, a love of pasta, overtaking the one in front, the mind and body working in harmony, it's a healthy thing to do. The list is endless... and do you believe that running is sensual? Whatever it is that makes the marathon different from other races, we may not be sure, but one thing that the marathon runner must have is the ability to tap into an inner strength, so where exactly does it come from and how does one access it? It's easy enough to say, "when the going gets tough..." but just how do the "tough get going"? Are we born with an inner strength? Obstinacy in the face of common sense? We certainly need it in the last six miles of a marathon because that inner strength allows you to push yourself to the limit and when you reach the limit you find that it's not an impenetrable barrier, a solid brick wall, but a door.

And when your thoughts turn to running a marathon, what do you look for? Do you consider only the 'London,' even though the chances of gaining an entry are slim, or do you look wider?

Every marathon has its own appeal and particular character so I believe it's wrong to make too many comparisons. How can you begin to compare the amazing and noisy atmosphere created at the London Marathon with the hilly and beautifully picturesque Seven Sisters

Marathon (now the Beachy Head) or Snowdon? On-road or off-road, flat or hilly, 30,000 or 20 runners – it doesn't matter because every marathon is special and excitingly different... and I recommend them all. To restrict oneself to just one marathon, the same one each year, is to only ever drink tea, only ever wear blue and only ever turn left when out driving.

As your number of marathons increases, in the midst of the variety of finishing times and weather conditions, the ever-present feel-good factor and quiet satisfaction from another milestone reached in easy and tough runs, there are things that happen, experiences that are lived and sensations that are felt, that fill the memory banks, standing out like gold nuggets in a prospector's pan of sand. They might be insignificant triflings or major happenings in a marathon yet they enrich the runner's life like nothing else.

I went to Ireland for a long weekend (five days actually) to run the **Dublin Marathon** and landed at Dublin airport in low mist thereby missing the chance of seeing a panoramic view of the city and getting a sense of its layout. I believed (quite wrongly) that the airport was to the south of the city (only 180° out, it is to the north) and the bus trip to the city centre did nothing to dispel my confused mind. The error was not realised until the following morning when the sun appeared to rise in the west causing my normally reliable sense of direction to never fully recover. The next day I went for a gentle jog, really just to give me a rough insight into the sort of conditions I might face in the marathon (a classic 'forewarned is forearmed' mentality.) In shorts and T-shirt, I set off in the rain and after about 40 minutes, when I was nearly back in the city centre, and it was still raining, I paused to check the tourist map that I was relying on. A local man who was walking towards me, stopped and shouted angrily, "Go home at once and put some clothes on!" then he stormed off. As for the marathon itself, I remember the friendly atmosphere, and running past what seemed like hundreds of houses with colourful Georgian front doors. Unfortunately, the race began rather ominously. I was brought to a standstill 300 yards after the start when my calf tightened and pulled. Against all common sense and because I'd come so far to run a marathon I did not give up but continued to run – well, jog – well jog, hobble and walk to begin with. The pain and awkwardness plateaued after a mile, so with only 25 miles to go, I decided to 'tough it out' and just run gently, finishing in 3:50, about an hour slower than my target time. How more or less memorable would the Dublin Marathon have been had that injury not happened, I don't know.

My only other overseas event was the **Caen Marathon** in Northern France in 1996. I can recall it being a very well-organised race with quite large but subdued crowds of 'watchers' (I found myself cheering them as I ran by). One psychological plus was the distance markers. They were big and bold and clearly visible and picked out each kilometre, not each mile. You would pass one of the markers and very quickly see the next one in the distance, giving you the feeling that you were getting round quite fast. The route went by some of the famous World War II Normandy beaches and Pegasus Bridge, which was a really emotional experience.

I ran the **Land's End Marathon** on the same weekend as the Hillsborough disaster and remember watching the terrible scenes on the TV in the hotel at Land's End. The following day, race day, was extremely windy – force nine, gusting ten. Add to that a very undulating course, and rain which became torrential, like a power shower, and you are left with an unforgettable experience. I ran 2:47 on that day, which was not my fastest but I rate it as my best marathon performance in terms of managing the conditions.

The sheer rugged beauty of the **Snowdon Marathon**, with its opening 4-mile climb up Llanberis Pass, the gravity-enriched section to half way and a very steep part near 23 miles before a ferocious descent into Llanberis was something that will stay in the memory but were those the most memorable bits? No, it was scoffing a whole packet of chocolate digestive biscuits afterwards and still feeling hungry that I remember most clearly. The **Suffolk-Essex Border Marathon** was a delightful off-road event that introduced me to crinkle-crankle walls. I'd never heard the term before but it was there on the route instructions sheet. Even though I didn't know what to look out for, when I saw it, I knew. The **Neolithic Marathon** begins in sight of the stone circles at Avebury and finishes 26.2 picturesque and challenging miles later, right by Stonehenge... stunning. The **Clarendon Way Marathon** links the two cathedral cities of

Winchester and Salisbury and is a must for all off-road fans. Was that where there were mixed showers at the finish on one occasion? Only those who were there in 1998 will know. The two-lap course of the **Taunton Marathon** in Somerset is on my 'specials' list because I ran it on no training. This was not an act of recklessness, stupidity or even forgetfulness but a practical attempt to discover how much of a part the mind plays in running a marathon. In my everyday life I am an optimist, a positive thinker and so I assured myself that I could run a marathon without any training. I did not even consider the baling-out option at 13 miles when the course passed by the finish at the end of the first lap. Neither did the absence of scrumpy at the drinks stations weaken my resolve. I just convinced my legs that I could do it, that after 83 marathons it was just a matter of doing it from memory and persuading the mind that I could hold a steady pace for 26.2 miles and, as usual, enjoy the marathon. My 3:47 that day was neither a PB nor a PW for me and I would certainly not recommend the idea to others but it proved a valuable point, that winning it 'upstairs' is crucial to running a marathon. Without a positive attitude, even adequate training will not guarantee you'll complete a marathon.

Just occasionally, ordinary runners can win marathons, which is why the **2-Piers Marathon** (Brighton Pier to Eastbourne Pier) stands out in my list of memories. So too, the **Tanner's Marathon** in Surrey but that was also because I finished more than 20 minutes ahead of the runner in second place. Getting lost on a marathon and adding extra, usually painful miles not only turns a marathon into an unplanned ultra but it also makes it extra special in the memory which is why **Rottingdean**, **Chanctonbury**, **Brentwood** and **Salisbury Marathons** are on my 'memorable' list.

The very flat inaugural **Worthing Marathon** was significant for me because it was where I first broke 3 hours. I ran the **South Coast Marathon** (Gosport) three times and on each occasion did so a week after running London with my finishing times showing very little depreciation, in fact in 1994 I actually ran Gosport faster.

I love the islands around Britain and have many special memories of running marathons on some of them. At the 1985 **Guernsey Marathon** I was on course to break 2:40 but had to settle for 2:44 and ninth place because of severe stomach cramp, possibly brought on by drinking water from one of the sponges because it was such a hot day but the real pleasure of that event was finishing only 20 seconds behind Ron Hill, one of my boyhood heroes. The **Isle of Man Marathon** is made particularly special if you indulge in all the races on offer (five in six days) like I did in 1999, i.e. Sunday – Marathon, Monday – 4-mile hill race, Tuesday – day off, Wednesday – 10 miles, Thursday – hilly 6 miles, Friday – another hilly 4-miler, making a total of 50 miles. My feelings about the two **Isle of Wight Marathons** and **Tresco Marathon (Isles of Scilly)** are found elsewhere in this book. The **Anglesey Marathon** is currently in my sights and I'd run a marathon on Lundy Island, Lindisfarne and the Goodwin Sands if there was one. My legs also like the idea of looking further afield and although the spirit is willing, the wallet is weak, otherwise exciting places such as the marathons in Reykjavik, Tromso (midnight sun), the Antarctic, Moscow, New Zealand and Hawaii would also have been done and T-shirted.

Is one marathon better or more worthy than another? I think not, although I have heard some people decry 'soft' marathons (whatever they are) suggesting that the more manly, rugged events are the proper marathons. So which is the toughest marathon? If that's not seen as a daft question it's certainly an unnecessary one. For instance, if I were to compare my course PBs for the **Seven Sisters** – 3:17, **Snowdon** – 3:23 and the **Rottingdean Windmill** – 3:35, achieved with a similar degree of fitness, I could assume from the figures that for me, the **Rottingdean Marathon** was the toughest. However, if pressed, I would have to say that the first time I ran the **Salisbury 5-4-3-2-1** event (August 2003) was my toughest marathon. I went badly off course on a very exposed part of the route and that added extra miles on a day when the temperature soared above 100°F, culminating in a PW to beat all others (more than double the worst of the figures above). I believe that it should only ever be light banter that argues which is the hilliest, flattest, most picturesque, fastest, most northerly, most drink stations and most popular marathon and we should tolerate the humour of which is the dullest, wettest, coldest, windiest, tallest, widest and twistiest marathons. That we all have different ideas as to which superlative defines a particular marathon is a strength of our sport. How dull and destructive it would be if there were only one correct answer.

Probably the most bizarre marathon I have ever run was the **Greenwich Foot Tunnel Marathon** in August 2002. Organised by the 100 Marathon Club to celebrate the hundredth anniversary of the tunnel, I was invited to be one of the hundred runners to take part.

Because the tunnel can be quite a busy underpass below the Thames the race had to start at 2am. The width of the tunnel, for those who don't know it, varies between 5 and 15 feet. It was like running in a large bent drainpipe! Each of the 56 laps that we had to do had a very tight U-turn at both ends of the tunnel. Thank goodness we didn't have to negotiate the steps as well. The popular and well-known marathon runner, Hugh Jones led all the way and when he finished in a Sunday morning jog time (for him) of 2:45 I still had 20 laps to go. The longitudinal profile of the tunnel is saucer-shaped in order to dip under the Thames and, roughly speaking is a 120-yard descent, 150-yard flat and 120-yard climb. Although there is a large fan at one end gently wafting in some air imagine the effect of the puffing and blowing of a hundred athletes in a confined space for up to five hours. After a while it felt like you were running through a cold sauna that had been filled with low-oxygen recycled damp air. It was truly an amazing experience, unique and definitely one for the memory banks. Look out for it again in the year 2102 when the tunnel will be celebrating its two-hundredth year, organised perhaps by the 200 Marathon Club. If you can't wait until then, there are other tunnel marathons, although you may have to travel abroad to find them.

There are so many marathons out there to enjoy, to captivate you and challenge you. They'll make enormous demands on your commitment, determination and honesty but the payback, the rewards are priceless. Whether you came to marathons courtesy of the London Marathon on television or through some unexplainable subconscious prompting, the resulting empowerment is without equal.

As for the subconscious 'out of the blue' inspiration to run, the thought process that unearthed the decision to go for a run is something we can only guess at. My own 'eureka' happened as mentioned back in the 70s on an unbelievably boring wet weekend. I was probably sitting in the lounge listening to either classical music or 60s pop (I had no TV). The brain, however, was alert – searching itself for something to cope with or overcome the situation. The electrical impulse that was dashing around the brain, looking for a solution had gone into a part of the brain that it may have never visited before. (For the average person, over 80 per cent of the brain doesn't get used) That's not to say that the 80 per cent is empty space. On the contrary, it's an enormous reservoir waiting to share its knowledge. Child prodigies, savants and exceptional, specialised talents arise from the brain impulses being a bit more adventurous and delving into unknown territory. So this electrical impulse of mine gatecrashes an unexplored field and comes away with the notion, "escape the boredom… run away… run…" It then reaches the conscious zone of my brain and I suddenly think, "I'm gonna go for a run."

That gatecrashed field could have been the one labelled 'cross-country running at school… great fun… good feeling after the run… sense of achievement… sense of achievement…'

It could also have been the field labelled 'primordial senses… save yourself… the present situation is not good… unproductive… save yourself… go somewhere else… run for it.'

Personally, I prefer the second field; the romantic image of the mystical lost world of our real beginning… instinct. This instinct zone, deep in the nether regions of the brain could also be the location of the inner strength on/off switch.

The appeal of marathon running could then be the result of the knock-on effect of a number of crucial factors, like a tumbling snake of dominoes (and just as unstoppable). The first domino being broadly described as **the urge to run** may not have been obviously successful the first time but there was probably a subconscious, positive reaction to it, an **adrenaline rush** that partly masked the pain and in doing so became the second domino. This would be the same domino that wavers, teeters, shall I, shan't I, and eventually falls forward to nudge domino number 3, another **urge to run** and then number 4, which could be called the **benefits of aerobic exercise** domino. The puffing and panting gives you loads of oxygen and courtesy of the perspiration process cleanses your system of impurities. Your body glows, not just from the physical exertion but also from an inner beauty and an increasing confidence and awareness. Runners exude inner beauty. Real beauty is not just skin deep. These are pretty powerful statements! but I believe they're true. Just look closely at runners as they finish an event, (I don't include the collapsing wreck who loses the plot as he/she staggers along Birdcage Walk and the Mall in the London Marathon) and you will see the inner person oozing strength, confidence… and beauty.

"It's summertime and the running is easy," a line nearly sung by hundreds of crooners for the last 60 years or so, might sum up the early stages of running enlightenment. Having survived the settling-in period, the realisation that running is enjoyable will prompt the appearance of more dominoes, **the will to improve**, a form of internal competitiveness will ask the question, "can I run further and can I run faster?" When you do run further you discover not only more about yourself but also more about the **immediate environment** in which you live. The beginner using the local park will begin to see it as an oasis of green where the runner-friendly trees not only give out crucial amounts of oxygen but as the seasons change, offer shade on burning hot days and shelter on rainy days. They'll also be markers to measure your fartlek sessions… because you decided that you do want to run faster as well. You'll meet other runners/joggers, initially via a nod or slight raising of a hand, an acknowledgement of 'me too' that develops into the domino labelled **camaraderie** and along with all the other dominoes prompts the one called **feeling of well-being**.

The knock-on effect is gaining momentum with each new domino, although the children's playground game of chain tag might now be a better analogy as you begin to accumulate important experiences. The abundance of fun runs and other races reach the ears, legs and brain and opens out one's internal competitiveness to the challenge of competing against others in a 10 km race. You set yourself the task of just completing it, or finishing it without walking, or managing it before darkness falls.

You succeed in perhaps 60:17, you weren't last and you weren't beaten by a rhinoceros carrying a ladder. You feel great! You glow. You have a shower and feel exhilarated. You recover. You bask in the praise from your friends, family and workmates the next day, but the day after that, the 60:17 gnaws at you. "I wonder..." and you do, you enter another 10 km event to try and beat the hour. You clock 58:30. You are hooked.

The domino of 'internal competitiveness' that you've already knocked over several times, now has a huge fluorescent banner above it with the words 'I can run further and I can run faster' flashing on it... and they're not dominoes anymore but huge heavy oak doors that collapse when you push them as if they're made of balsa wood.

10 km becomes 10 miles and 10-minute miling becomes 9 then 8 and 7. The half marathon beckons and is duly conquered, then you plateau out for a while, but not for too long, because you'd already thought about the 'biggie' a few months earlier.

You take your running gear on holiday and discover the thrill of running on sandy beaches, up mountains and exploring new routes. You don't buy tourist maps but Ordnance Survey ones because they show the footpaths, towpaths and bridleways that will open up the whole world. They will also open up the main reason for being able to build up a solid foundation of **stamina**, **strength** and **time on your feet**, sufficient to run marathons. Running off road is for most runners the bulk of their training and has in my mind a double whammy effect. The conscious response is the feeling of escaping from civilisation, tarmac roads and pavements and all other elements of the concrete jungle and modern world. Paths that are gravel or grass are obviously softer on the legs, replacing the continuous, injurious jarring of road running with giving and forgiving surfaces. Soft, uneven ground massages the foot almost like reflexology by stimulating the acupoints on the soles of the feet. I used to find the famous cobbles in the London Marathon a pleasant relief from the GBH of the streets of the capital and similarly, I would jump at the opportunity in any road marathon to run on a grass verge. Even 100 yards of such a surface can be just the rest the legs need. If marathons were only ever run on roads, our sport would certainly not be as popular as it is. In the year of the foot and mouth epidemic, when runners were obliged to replace their usual off-road training with road running, it may have been a coincidence, but runners' times in the London Marathon that year seemed to be generally much slower.

When running on a beach, by a canal or river, through woodlands or over hills and mountains you'd have to be a blinkered racehorse not to be affected by the beauty of such environments. Who can fail to enjoy the changing panoramic views of the countryside as you run by and the variety of birds, animals and insects that abound? I have been stopped in my tracks by the sight of hypnotic, delicately coloured azure blue butterflies, graceful white egrets, or green woodpeckers screeching their annoyance for being disturbed. I've also come across an emu, escaped from a local zoo and even a black wild boar when running in Normandy, France.

The subconscious effect, the second part of the double whammy, is the innate response, our built-in reaction to freedom. The junior section of my club, the Seaford Striders, frequently meets at different venues to do their running. Fortunately, we have the South Downs on our doorstep offering limitless scope and expanse. Their reaction to the freedom is an inspiring sight. As one parent put it recently, "it's primeval," as he watched his son and fifty other children run excitedly down an inviting grassy slope into the Cuckmere Valley. I can climb over the fence at the end of my back garden and immediately be on the edge of the South Downs and able to access an endless myriad of inviting runner-friendly footpaths, fields and bridleways. This sort of 'green carpet treatment' far exceeds that of the red variety and is in my mind the main reason why we continue to run.

More dominoes/oak doors called **escapism, the beautiful countryside, pain, stubbornness** and **adventure** appear and are knocked over, which is very important because you will need them all and a few more besides, to run the marathon, whether you are a novice or seasoned athlete. Hopefully, somewhere within the long months of training and lesser races, you are also developing and honing the extra talents that will help you survive the emotional roller coaster of the final six miles of a marathon.

Coping with the physical demands is something that perhaps 50 per cent of the population could manage. I refer to our skeletal muscles and the two fibre types – fast twitch and slow twitch. We all have both types but the proportion of each will vary from muscle to muscle and person to person. However, evidence supports the opinion that your fibre type distribution is inherited. In other words, we are born marathon runners... or not. Slow twitch muscles as the name suggests react slowly to physical activity. They exert less force and can easily cope with prolonged bouts of exercise without exhaustion, which is ideal for endurance-based sports. They ensure the legs receive a continuous rich supply of blood to enable efficient production of aerobic energy.

Athletes with dominant fast twitch muscles are the sprinters of the world. Characteristically their muscle fibres are large and strong, react quickly and forcefully but are easily exhausted. One of my former pupils at Newlands School in Seaford, East Sussex – Jason Hussain – epitomises the fast twitch, explosive power of sprinters. By the age of 18 he had reduced his PB for 200 metres to 21.43 seconds and whenever I saw him run, time and the other runners appeared to stand still as he powered his way to victory with what seemed like effortless ease. In his training, he would probably not run further than 1 km at one go but if that seems worlds apart from our marathon preparation there are similarities between us and sprinters. The runners' 'high' that I selfishly thought was only a distance-runners' enjoyment is present in short races too. Perhaps like twitching muscles one can experience either a fast high or a slow high but it was when Jason chatted to me about the camaraderie (that's fast camaraderie, not slow) among sprinters that I realised several of our 'dominoes' are also part of his armoury. Maybe not adventure but pain; not escapism but stubbornness, and definitely present is the surfers' factor (see later paragraph for explanation of this last term). But I can't help thinking that the enjoyment factor, which for marathon runners goes on for hours is, when it comes to sprinters, comparable with eating a malteser.

In trying to explain why so many marathon runners repeatedly put their body (and mind) through an event that, whatever their level of fitness, does involve a degree of pain, my brother-in-law, Warner Wallace, has an interesting notion. He runs for the Forest Edge Footers, a small running club near Fordingbridge in Hampshire, and likens the runner to the surfer who keeps putting to sea in search of the 'perfect wave'.

For the runner, the perfect wave is the day when everything goes well. When the weather and temperature are just right or are easily conquered. As the miles fly by, the route, the spectators, the drinks stations all seem to harmonise with your needs. You run like a well-oiled machine from the start. You are poetry in motion as you settle into the perfect pace, which is comfortable but not too casual. You feel good and know that you've read the conditions right. It's certainly not an easy run because you are working hard but your body is responding. The low point that you usually experience even on a good day fails to appear. You feel strong as you cruise past the 20-mile point and sense something special. Your pace is good yet you are aware that you have plenty in reserve and you could run faster… and you do. There is pain but it fades. You finish fast, fresh and buoyant. Is that the perfect wave? Maybe… but you'll no doubt run another marathon in case it isn't. The perfect wave does not necessarily mean your fastest marathon so perhaps it's just another way of describing one's competitiveness or search for something that either can't be achieved or doesn't exist anyway.

Sometimes it is fun to use the stubbornness and cavalier attitude that is a hallmark of a marathon runner to face the challenge of the various 'character' events that exist round the country and there can be none more in need of the marathon runner's grittiness than the **Tough Guy Challenge** on a frosty morning in late January, just outside Wolverhampton. But only enter it if you are not put off by walking, wading and swimming through ice-topped puddles, lakes and rivers, running over burning hay bales, crawling along icy drainage tunnels, squelching through enough mud to ensnare a battleship, coping with zip wires, rope ladders, electric wire, tightrope walking, squirming under wire netting and climbing over huge hayricks. In other words, surviving what they creatively call 'the killing fields.'

The age at which people continue to be involved in competitive sport varies widely with each discipline. Famously, Stanley Matthews was still playing professional league football (for Stoke City) at the age of 52 and there are many examples of men playing 'park' football to an even greater age. Other sports like badminton, cricket, golf and cycling can claim even larger numbers of 'pensioners' still actively and energetically involved in their sport.

It wasn't so long ago that it was unthinkable that anyone of pensionable age would be running a marathon yet it was partly because of this that Madge Sharples shot to fame in the first **London Marathon**. The cameras picked out her smiling, cheerful face as she ambled round the course and when statisticians in the commentary box informed viewers that she was 63, a star was born.

My aunt, Grace Bulger, was 69 when her doctor advised her to take more exercise to stave off arthritis. She had been a seamstress in her working life and had done very little in the way of physical activity. Her son, Howard, was a member of the New Forest Runners in Hampshire so she went along to his club one evening and happened to link up with a few other older ladies. Over the next few months she discovered a liking for jogging, and enjoyed it even more the further she ran. This led to Grace running her debut marathon at London in 1990 at the age of 70, recording a time of under 5 hours.

The running boom of the 80s unearthed a huge enthusiasm for marathons and that interest has been sustained and grown older, creating a situation where veteran categories not only outnumber younger groups in some events but also outperform them sometimes.

So, why do we run marathons when we are past our 'sell by date' and unlikely to set a PB? My marathon PB was set more than 18 years ago (over 100 marathons ago) and my perfect wave was the day I ran the South Downs Way 80 miles in 12 hours 42 minutes (and that was ten years ago) yet for me, the enjoyment and sense of achievement factor is still as strong as ever. Having broken the 3-hour barrier 25 times, trying to keep under 4 hours is now my time challenge for a road marathon or just being able to finish feeling strong and satisfied. As for off-road events, the time is really irrelevant and instead, completing it without getting lost often becomes the goal.

Providing we look after our bodies by eating wisely, wearing the right sort of running shoes and doing whatever exercises are necessary to maintain flexibility, we should be able to continue running marathons well into our dotage, long after other sportsmen and women may have thrown in the towel or hung up their water wings.

Another factor that might make running unique in the sporting world is the ambient blend of competitiveness and friendliness. Whether I'm taking part in low-key fun runs or competitive races, marathons or 10 kms, I am not only cheered by the members of my club but also I get genuine encouragement from other club runners, their supporters and the marshals and neutral crowds too. Can you see that happening in many other sports?

It is believed by many that an athlete should be able to run 10 miles and, with training, could run 20. Running beyond that distance however, requires skills that are not athletic in origin. When I was setting PBs at all distances (many years ago) I could run 10 km races in 33 minutes but it never seemed to be the best I could do. However, when it came to 10-mile events, on those occasions that I recorded 55 minutes, it felt as though I was running close to the limit of my physical strength and stamina. So too, over half marathons and 20-mile races, but I quickly learnt that the last 6 miles of a marathon demanded something else to sustain me. It needed mental endurance, a tough, cast iron will and, in the case of my first 26.2 miles, an extra reason to complete it – fund raising for charity. A first marathon can be successful with the right preparation, choosing the right pace for the conditions and a slice of luck.

I don't know what percentage of marathon first-timers survive the experience and the physically painful aftermath and mental exhaustion, and then as in all previous lesser distance races wonder if they could do it quicker. If you run a second marathon, there's a strong chance that you'll do a third and fourth. Then with the mindset of a surfer you'll go off in pursuit of the perfect wave.

There were many factors that contributed to running your first marathon and a few more reasons why you ran numbers two and three. When you venture past three and beyond ten it must be because of some very powerful motivation but the pursuit of PBs certainly isn't one of them or if it is, it's one that won't last. You may reach ten or twenty still believing that your PB can be reduced even further. Your first sub-4, for instance, is a mental milestone, a personal triumph, but it's soon forgotten in your next marathon when you lower your PB by 13 minutes. Perhaps your brain spots that 13 is half of 26 so you work out, with primary school maths, that you must have been running 30 seconds a mile faster. You might then ponder what your PB would be if you could run each marathon mile 10 seconds faster still… and if you could, what would you have to do to achieve it. You think about doing one more training run each week, going out twice in one day, trying out fartlek sessions. You might time yourself in reaching a certain point along one of your regular routes then every now and again try to reach the same point quicker or perhaps you see how far along that same route you could get in 30 minutes; then next time, try to run further in the same measured time. All the while you're improving your technique, preparation and strength, running more and more marathons and chasing PBs, other factors are becoming inextricably embedded in your psyche, influences that will take over when PBs become a thing of the past.

My third marathon broke 3 hours and from then on I set my sights on a sub 2:40 time, which used to be the qualifying time for London. It was also approximately 6-minute miling, which for someone who liked facts and figures, meant that I was able to while away many a mile doing sums in my head to calculate a likely finishing time. After 23 marathons I ran 2:41 over the undulating **New Forest Marathon** course and that should have led to me achieving my sub 2:40 goal over a flatter course but sadly, it never did. But for that lazy streak in me which restricted my training to rarely running over 50 miles a week, I'm sure I could have been chasing down a sub 2:30 time. I can hardly believe that when I ran my fastest marathon I was running 6 minutes 10 seconds for each mile yet now I can't manage even one mile at that pace. Eventually I remind myself that I must grow slow gracefully and just continue to enjoy the sensation of being able to finish a marathon feeling good, regardless of the time on the race clock. However slow I am now, it doesn't remove the fact that there once was a time when I ran 2:41. And there's another point. How often do we feel annoyed when we've had a bad race? We look to blame tired legs or injuries that have impeded our usual pace, the hills that seem tougher than the last time… whatever it is that has caused us to have a bad run and set a PW we can so easily become unfairly critical of ourselves. The strong determination within us that enables us to get round 26.2 miles in a marathon seems now unable to see the whole picture. It's at times like this that we need to remind ourselves that the ability to run a marathon is an exceptional human skill, a talent that could place us in the top 1 per cent of the population. Isn't that good enough? I think that it's important to see our marathon running for what it is – a magnificent human achievement, whether we do it faster than before, reasonably well, OK, slowly or with a painful struggle.

I remember attending a talk by Gordon Pirie, that superb international athlete of the 50s and 60s, who kept his audience enthralled with his reminiscences, opinions and advice however, he did have a reputation for outspoken and sometimes provocative views and it certainly surfaced when he suggested that everyone should be able to run a sub-2:30 marathon – it was just a matter of application and commitment. As his talk was on the eve of one of the New Forest Marathons it caused quite a stir among the audience, which consisted mainly of competitors who were mentally preparing themselves for the following day's race. I'd like to believe him but when I think of my attempts to reduce my PB and the same determined efforts that other marathon runners who I know well have made, I find it very hard to agree with him. It does seem that we all have a natural 'limit' to our aspirations, one that can be physical or mental... or both. How many runners get stuck on 3:02 or 4:01 for instance and can't, whatever they do, find the 'umph' to break through what is, after all, only a time barrier? Was it the frustration of such an artificial hurdle that caused Roger Ockenden, a contributor to this book, to give up running marathons? What often makes one's pursuit of a PB more painful and demoralizing is the paradox that the stronger and faster you run and the nearer to your limit you get, the closer you get to sustaining an injury. Our competitiveness and ruthless determination, those traits that marathon runners need loads of, can be our downfall, making us overconfident and convinced that you can go faster and further but sometimes with heartbreaking results.

I've done more than a hundred marathons since my fastest time yet my enjoyment factor could not be higher and I can often measure my own degree of enjoyment of marathon running by my reaction to being unable to take part in one because of, say, injury. Can you bear to watch the **London Marathon** on TV knowing that but for misfortune you would be there too?

"Look at that sea of smiling faces, it's just not fair. Sod the injury," I might say to myself, then swear at the budgie or kick the aspidistra...! Or, if I'm really annoyed or really badly injured, I persuade the budgie to kick the aspidistra. The enforced lay-off, however, can be seen as a good thing sometimes, although I'd refuse to admit it at the time. If I manage the break from running with wisdom and determination I could emerge from it much stronger (absence makes the mind more determined). Because there are marathons on nearly every weekend, somewhere in the country or one flight away, it is very easy to forget to give yourself a closed season, a fallow month, a period when you can re-charge your batteries and hopefully run wiser and better. To paraphrase a famous quotation, 'Some runners are wise... some are otherwise.'

It is interesting to see the different ways that runners respond to completing a marathon and what they do immediately after crossing the finishing line. Perhaps the most bizarre and regularly seen sequence is the runner who, on seeing the FINISH banner, fills his lungs with oxygen, steps up a gear or two and storms home like an express train in a hurry, his face a brief picture of ecstatic delight and then overwhelming relief... which slowly transforms into grimaces and a shocked expression. He desperately tries to keep up the outward feeling of elation as he walks along the funnel to have the medal draped round his neck. He then walks less easily to the drinks table, wishing it weren't so far away (about 8 metres actually). He stands still... fatal! Whatever you do, don't stand still because it's then that your legs will say "Aha, we've stopped, that means I've got you round and we've finished. Thank goodness. I'm switching the lights off now... goodnight!" At this point the ability to move (never mind to run) drains quicker than a pint of beer down a dry throat on a hot sunny day. He should of course be going for a gentle warm-down run to shake out those tired muscles, flush out the lactic acid from the calves and quads, relax and unwind... restore one's equilibrium... Get real, he's done for and going nowhere! How strange that one moment he was flying high on adrenaline... surfing the crest of an invincible wave... and 10 seconds later he is a beached whale with rigor mortis. 'Mind over matter' had got him to the finishing line but the 'matter' which had baled out more than five miles ago has now been joined by the 'mind', sensing that the journey is done, the game is over, the ignition key has been turned irreversibly... to off.

The two extreme images in the sequence are so incredibly different that it seems inconceivable they are separated by no more than seconds. I've been there, done that and got the cramp occasionally myself but most times have thankfully been able to control my pace so that I could finish strongly **and** enjoy the sensations of the post race experience. Take a drink as soon after finishing as possible and eat the banana, apple or snack bar that's in your goody bag but don't whatever you do, stand still. If it's not cold or raining, cheer others home, keep walking and jog a few paces, gently massage your legs, wriggle your toes and stay conscious because the more active you are in the hours after you've finished the easier and quicker will be your recovery.

I believe that all marathon runners are competitive people, if not so much against other runners, then in the way they challenge themselves. Extending one's boundaries of speed or distance, or both, is probably what led many to run a marathon and may be another clue as to why we run them because it can quite naturally lead to a sense of running with, rather than against, one's fellow competitors... and that's just one small step towards one of the most powerful factors in marathon running – camaraderie – the feeling of 'in it together' and of helping each other through the difficult moments as well as sharing the good times. And could some of those occasions in a marathon when 'all is well with the world' also be down to the picturesque scenery that the route is taking you through? And do runners only notice the surroundings when they're not focused on chasing a PB or are just plain struggling? I don't think so! I have yet to run a marathon whose course hasn't helped me in some way, whether it be running over Tower Bridge in the London Marathon or past a line of giant redwoods in the New Forest; running close to my limit or ambling along with no regard for my speed. If anyone doubts the importance of the 'views' when running a marathon, try running 26.2 miles on a treadmill in a room with four bare walls, no windows and no external stimuli.

Chapter 3

Marathon Reviews

The Tresco Marathon

The wisdom of looking further afield than the London Marathon was never clearer for me than when I was rejected for London 2002. I chose instead to enter the Tresco Marathon (Isles of Scilly) and being on the same day as London it meant that I could train alongside my fellow Seaford Striders who were preparing for London.

The pre-race information for the Tresco marathon told me that it was 7.5 laps of the Island. My first thought was one of uncertainty and trepidation, and how I might cope with the repetition. However, I sent off my entry form and booked a weekend break on the Island.

I caught the morning ferry from Penzance and settled myself in a comfortable seat with a good view of the Cornish coast. The first sign that it was going to be a special weekend came not from the warm welcome I received from one of the organisers while on the ferry but from the unofficial greeting party, in the shape of a school of dolphins that criss-crossed ahead of the bow of the ship. We docked at St Mary's, the main island, before being transported by a craft the size of a very small fishing boat to Tresco. I received another warm greeting when I stepped onto the minute stone jetty near the south-western end of the Island and was escorted in one of the few permitted vehicles (it was more like a golfing buggy) to the Island Hotel. When I caught sight of it I thought I had died and gone to heaven. Built of local stone it was almost camouflaged amongst the rugged coastline on the leeward side of the Island with a 'front row seat' to a beach that must rate as one of the most beautiful in the world.

The shallow waters between the islands clearly show the white rock of the seabed. This creates white sandy beaches and when the sun is out, the sea becomes a breath-taking turquoise blue.

As for the marathon itself, which attracts just over one hundred competitors, every person on the island turns out to watch, armed with a list of the runners' names and numbers. As the race gets underway the 7.5 laps begins to show itself as a bonus, not a drawback. The spectators soon learn to put a name to the faces they keep seeing and cheer you as if they have known you all your life (bonus No 1). With four drinks stations every lap (of 3.5 miles) that's more than London can boast (bonus No 2) and they offer a very wide choice of drinks and snacks (bonus No 3). If they haven't got your particular need, then I'm sure they could have it ready for you on the next lap. As for bonus No 4, each twist and turn of the route reveals more beautiful scenery and you are drawn along in expectation of the next image of nature at its best. I'm sure that I was not the only one who contemplated doing an extra lap just to see it all again.

Martin Bulger

The New Forest Marathon

Of all the marathons that I have run, the New Forest Marathon is without doubt my favourite. Is that because I set my marathon PB of 2:41 there in 1987, or perhaps it's the excellent organisation and friendly support? Could it be the challenging route or the sheer beauty of the forest? Although I live in East Sussex, I was born in the New Forest area and so maybe it feels like I'm back home. The truth is, it's my favourite for probably all of those reasons.

I do feel very lucky that I have been able to do every New Forest Marathon since the first one in 1983. At the time of writing that's all 25 marathons (at an average of 3:20). I may be the only one in the world to have achieved this, I'm not sure.

If you decide to run the 'New Forest', don't ride the ponies that you come across because they don't know the way. Look the other way when you run past the four pubs (unless you've got money in your bum bag) and soak up the atmosphere and beauty of the trees... and only overtake me if you have to.

In the early years, The Ringwood Pipe Band would have led you up Station Road in New Milton to the start line and as for the race, the first few miles are fast and fairly flat. You will then enjoy the easiness of the downhill part towards the 3-mile point and feel comfortable as you breeze along the flat stretch past 4 miles. Breathe in the oxygen-rich air as you cruise and weave through the trees past 6, 7 and 8 miles and you will feel at one with nature. You will love the comradeship and camaraderie of your team-mates or total strangers who just happen to be running at your pace. They'll lift your spirits and carry you beyond the halfway stage.

Take your mind off the pounding of your feet on the hard road at 14 and 15 miles and look around at the incredibly tall and majestic trees standing as a guard of honour along Rhinefield and feel humble beside such giants of nature. Then a few pangs of doubt may creep into your mind as you run along the seemingly endless approach to 16 and 17 miles and your thirst will demand the Atlantic.

"Why am I doing this?" you may say to yourself as you stare at the long drawn out climb past 19 miles, and at 20 your senses could produce feelings of hate for the customers who stand outside the pub drinking nectar and eating banquets in a roll. But then you think poetically, "Hang on a mo! there's only 10 km to go." So you take out your mental notebook and calculate a likely finishing time (forgetting the 3 climbs to come).

You'll pass more drinkers outside The Plough as you thump down and up the last steep bit at 23 miles but then you'll inwardly cheer at the thought of the 3 flat miles to the finish. When you turn into Stem Lane you should begin to smell the finishing line. There's a final drinks station by the 25-mile point and the adrenaline kicks in (again). Your spirit is lifted and you quicken your pace knowing that you've cracked it. You overtake someone and that gives you the energy to overtake the next runner and before you know where you are, you're storming along to the finish like the previous 26 miles hadn't happened.

Martin Bulger

The Seven Sisters (Beachy Head) Marathon

Once, this was as difficult to gain a place in as the London Marathon yet the two events could not be more different. Runners only have to stand on the start line besides St Bede's School in Eastbourne and look up at an angle of 45° at the first 200 metres of the course to get an idea of the challenge that lies ahead. Too many runners however, with energy to waste, will try to run up the steep incline while others, with wisdom, adopt a brisk walk mentality. When the route levels out, after 800 metres, the difference between the foolhardy or talented runner and the wise brisk walkers will be no more than about 150 yards but the energy lost in gaining such a small, futile advantage will come back to haunt many of the runners later on. Those with the confidence and self-control will let 60 or 70 runners overtake them on the opening climb but will pull them in and more as the event unfolds. As the popular former organiser, Leslie Smith would say, "This is not a race but a challenge."

At the top of that first climb a lone piper will be playing to you, encouraging you with his distinctive melodies. As you follow the ridge towards Butt's Brow, with a superb panoramic view over Eastbourne to your right and the beautiful Downlands to your left, you will feel at peace with the world. You'll soon descend into Jevington then need to find the most economical pace that will carry you up to the top of the next ridge. Once there, gravity will again run with you as you snake downwards through Friston Forest and you'll feel great and powerful once more but knowing in the back of your mind that what comes down must go up... and up... and up to Windover Hill. From here, you can see the English Channel in one direction, the North Downs inland to your right, the South Downs stretching away as far as the eye can see ahead of you... and if you're carrying a radio in your bum bag you'll be able to pick up Radio Tibet. The friendly and much needed check point near Alfriston will recharge your batteries and help you to conquer the next big climb, up to Bo Peep and another ridge path. From here, savour the moment as you cruise (effortlessly) towards 'High and Over' and Litlington. Here it will seem like the whole village has turned out to feed you, play music to you or just cheer you on and up the next knee-trembling slope. The fifty energy-sapping steps near Charleston Manor is, I think, meant to prepare you for the infamous and debilitating steps at West Dean. A sign advising you "lift out of action, please use the stairs," will bring a smile to your face but the previous 19 miles will quickly wipe away the smile as you dig deep into your stubbornness to reach the top, but it's worth it for the view when you get there, that of the meandering river in the Cuckmere Valley. Strangely, there are nine ups and downs to negotiate when traversing the Seven Sisters cliffs. But yet again, the runner is lifted by the welcome expertise of another strategic check point, this time at Birling Gap. As you leave it reluctantly, your legs weary from 22 miles of more changes of altitude than a Grand Canyon bungee jumper, you look ahead at the sting in the tail. To begin with, it (Beachy Head) doesn't look a serious problem. The path appears to be level but your leg muscles know otherwise. Beyond Belle Tout you'll ascend as best as you can the undulations that unkindly go up more than they come down. Then the route finally flattens out and you know that you've cracked it because you are at the top of Beachy Head and from there every route is downwards. If you've saved something for a good finish, now is the time, with just a mile to go, to enjoy the downhill dash to the finishing line, but beware the last 40 metres. The path suddenly becomes a near vertical drop of about 20 feet... just what your jelly legs don't want. Survive that nerve-wracking moment and you'll thoroughly deserve the medal, which considering the 20 or more climbs and corresponding descents, ought to be an engraved yoyo. This marathon is 26.2 miles of stunning scenery. It's fairly tough but with much of the route being on muscle-friendly grass, you'll find that you recover from it much quicker than after running a normal road marathon.

Martin Bulger and Brian Winn

The Isle of Wight Marathon

This long-running event on the east of the Island owes its longevity (50 years) to the expertise of its organisers – Ryde Harriers – and it being a most challenging course. It is run entirely on roads and is, apart from the flat opening 1.5 miles and closing half mile, classically and continuously undulating, adding up to 1,505 feet of ascent. This does not give the runner very much help in settling into a rhythm, which is perhaps why this marathon is sometimes referred to as the 'tough one.' Held in May of each year, it's just a 15-minute ferry trip from Portsmouth and boasts Mark Pickard (2:22) and Lesley Watson (2:52) as the course record holders. The route is open to traffic, which might suggest to those who haven't run it that it could be dangerous but whether it's due to the road marshals and police support or tolerance of the drivers on the island, the marathon has a very good safety record. Perhaps after 50 years, marathon runners making their way along the roads around the east of the island have become such an accepted and well-known sight that they are given the space and respect that they warrant. The two laps of Ryde Boating Lake at the start serve as a good 'loosener' but don't really prepare you for the climb out of Ryde or the ups and downs of the next 10 km. Passing through the county town of Newport the route heads due south in pursuit of more undulations then shortly after reaching picturesque Godshill, turns east. Here your confidence might receive a boost when you see the 15-mile marker and your navigational instincts make you feel as though you are at last heading back towards Ryde.

Shanklin and Sandown seem to be quickly pulled in but there are still some challenging climbs to overcome in the last 6 miles. Wherever you are on the course you are always in sight of a much higher hill than the one you're trying to conquer, and that ought to help you in the mind-battle that you are fighting. Also, although the course is fairly rural, there is surprisingly good crowd support throughout, again, probably due to a feeling of tradition that has built over the 50 years.

At 24 miles, you sense there are no more tough sections as the route levels out for a while then drops down to the seafront, to leave you with another lap of the lagoon to the finish. It is a fairly tough marathon and requires disciplined running, pacing yourself in order to survive the undulations, and a rock-hard determination to stay focused. Every marathon that you enter will challenge you; this one will really challenge you.

Martin Bulger

The Needles XC Marathon

If you're not particularly concerned about chasing a PB, preferring instead the opportunity to cruise through beautiful countryside, over varied terrain on a warm, sunny day, I recommend the Needles XC Marathon. It's the Isle of Wight's other marathon, courtesy of the West Wight Road Runners and is fast establishing itself as the race to do, and one that boasts a challenging course and stunning scenery all the way round the route. This marathon really epitomises everything that is appealing about our sport. It is organised by runners for runners and they have intentionally devised a route that takes in some of the loveliest parts of the island, parts that they, as local residents, train on regularly and want to share with others. Make it a long weekend or part of a memorable holiday and you will be captivated by the magic of the island.

This marathon, which is 90 per cent off-road, is best reached by taking the short ferry trip from Lymington across the Solent to Yarmouth. You'll find a warm, friendly welcome, excellent facilities and a fairly small field of runners gathering for the start of the race at the West Wight Sports Centre.

The course begins on road but soon becomes a track and footpath heading north towards Kings Manor Farm and along Freshwater Way, close to the River Yar. Arriving at the first checkpoint you'll be distracted by the view back across the Solent to Keyhaven and Lymington and feel you could reach out and touch Hurst Castle. You will then have a 'front row seat' to enjoy the famous narrow waterway and the plethora of marine craft as you jog the waters-edge path to Colwell Bay and Totland Bay. The route then leaves the coast briefly and climbs steeply to Headon Warren and you are drawn on in expectation of the next spectacular view. Right on cue as you begin to descend, is Alum Bay, famous for its rainbow-coloured sands and ahead, The Needles – the chalk stacks and lighthouse that stand proud as the guardians of the western end of the Isle of Wight. If there is any wind, it will be on your back as the course turns east, helping you to run like a free spirit along West High Down and past Tennyson's Monument to Freshwater Bay. Every step you take is there to savour and delight as the soft, runner-friendly grass makes you feel like you're running on air, successfully concealing just how much climb there really is. In every direction, there is the beauty of nature – seascapes and ever-changing coastlines, woodland and downland, flora and fauna – causing the miles to fly by almost unnoticed. Run the Tennyson Trail up onto Compton Down then follow the Hamstead Trail as it takes you across the island, through lush fields and dense woodland to checkpoint 4 and you will have covered 19 miles. Then, for a while the course is flat. Willow trees abound as you traverse the water meadows around the inlets of Newtown Quay. Once again the route runs close to the Solent and there should be an unexpected spring in your stride as part of you senses that you are at last heading towards the finish. Skip along the winding path through Bouldnor Forest to checkpoint 5 and when the course joins the old disused railway line there's only 2 miles to go. As you walk, jog or run this last section, past the reed beds that border the River Yar, you may begin to regret that the race is almost over. Only your tired legs will yearn for the finishing line. And when you reach it, there'll be warm applause from the spectators and all those who finished ahead of you and stayed around to support their fellow runners. Later, you'll return to the mainland, taking with you the memory of almost more beautiful sights and sounds than is possible to cram into one marathon.

Martin Bulger

City of Salisbury 5-4-3-2-1 Marathon

The unusual numerical suffix to the Salisbury Marathon is not as it might seem, the countdown that the official starter yells into his megaphone. Nor is it the number of inches in a marathon but simply the fact that there are 5 rivers to cross, 4 hills to climb, 3 country estates to run through and 2 castles and 1 cathedral to admire as you pass them. Put your PB calculator away and replace it with a camera.

This marathon is an off-road gem, shining emerald green with splashes of golden corn in the August sunshine. Organised by the Salisbury Fire Service it attracts up to 500 social runners and walkers who can choose from several different distances. Don't expect noisy crowds but instead treat your ears to nature's infinitely more pleasing birdsong, babbling brooks and the sound of wind in the trees.

The low key, relaxed "off you go then" gets the marathon underway and you follow the River Avon upstream for a mile or so then climb the hill to Old Sarum Castle. Pause to take in the fabulous view of Salisbury and its famous cathedral spire then skirt the eastern boundary of the city along the easy-to-run ridge separating the Avon and Bourne valleys. Follow part of the Clarendon Way (a snippet of another delightful marathon) across a huge field where, if it's hot and sunny, you'll be glad of the tree cover when the route goes serenely through the forest surrounding Clarendon House. Then in no time at all you'll be running towards the incredibly beautiful Longford Castle and wishing you had brought your camera. Enjoy this easy running section of the course across the broad flat river valley because very soon you'll have to negotiate the 350-feet climb to Clearbury Ring which will severely tax even the most ardent fan of off-road running. There's a field that seems to go on for ever... and on a hot day, it goes further than that. The path is badly rutted, flint-strewn, nettled, with aggressive spiky corn or maize stubble or plants that are head-high and still growing. If you're a true marathon runner you'll grit your teeth, steady your nerve and search your cranium for the brain cell that provides runners with the degree of obstinacy that is needed at moments like this.

You'll probably recover your composure on the next stretch then marvel at running through an enchanted forest of ancient yew trees that can conjure up all manner of images of woodland mysteries from centuries gone by. You'll find your way out thanks to a ball of blue string – echoes of the story in Greek mythology of how Theseus, father of Aegeus, escaped from the Labyrinth. When you arrive at checkpoint number 7, which just happens to be in the Fox and Goose Public House car park in Coombe Bissett you will be sorely tempted to refresh the parts that carbo drinks cannot reach. Whatever your tipple, you'll need that obstinate brain cell again because there is another mean hill, a mile-long climb up Drove Lane towards Salisbury Racecourse. It's here that the 30 km competitors turn right and make a bee-line for the cathedral spire while the marathon runners turn left. As you go in the opposite direction to the one you'd prefer you may have second thoughts but then the confidence returns when you find yourself cruising downhill through picturesque woodland and over easy-to-run fields all the way to Wilton.

Unless you know the route, you will have been relying on matching the map route with the written commentary to avoid getting lost... like I did twice in 2003. It certainly helps to develop the skill of keeping one eye on the path in front of you, one eye on the map and one eye on the written instructions... or persuade yourself that it's OK to stop every so often to check the map. Thankfully, the last 5 miles through Quidhampton, Lower Bemerton and Harnham are flat and just when you feel as though you've had enough of the beautiful Wiltshire countryside, you'll jog under the grey stone arch of the South Gate, turn right and find yourself running past Salisbury Cathedral. Crowds of tourists with their eyes transfixed on greater things will not notice the weary runners weaving their way past them. The route leaves the cathedral grounds at North Gate and takes you through the City centre and as long as you follow the river path you'll finish where you started. This is definitely not a fast marathon but it has all that you'd expect of an off-road event in abundance. Run with someone and share the navigating. Run with a bum bag to hold money for the pub pit stop, spare drink and a camera. Run the Salisbury 5-4-3-2-1 Marathon... it's a gem.

Martin Bulger

The Yakima River Canyon Marathon

To the east of Seattle, which is in the top left-hand corner of the USA, is the Cascade Mountain Range. One of the many rivers that cut their way through the mountains is the Yakima as it descends inland towards the Columbia basin. As part of my personal challenge to run a marathon in each of the 52 states of America, the one I chose to represent the state of Washington (not DC) was the Yakima River Canyon Marathon. I have now run it 4 times since its inaugural event in 2001 and without doubt it must rate as my favourite marathon out of the 240-plus that I have done so far.

It is run in early April when the temperatures are generally below 10°C and the course is not easy. Race directors Bob and Lenora Dolphin do a fantastic job in organising a superb marathon and it attracts 400–500 runners, including a significant percentage from around the world. The event really starts on the Friday when you can collect your race packet and all the information you'll need to complete the race. This is followed by a very nice pre-race pasta meal when you can listen to great guest speakers. The canyon is a bit remote so there is a bus to take you to the start. There are no cars or other vehicles allowed in the canyon during the race so all the competitors have to use the bus. The race begins at 8am and has a time limit of 7 hours so it is possible to walk most of the course and still complete the course in time. Because the canyon is so remote, you will not see many people on the course other than at the aid stations. The marathon is started by a whistle from a train then, strangely, the race begins with you running in what seems to be the wrong direction; instead of facing the canyon, you are heading back up the road but it does turn soon and makes its way into the canyon. The route contains two small loops, which means that you don't run the full length of the canyon. This is fortunate because at the far end the road rises very steeply, so cutting it out is perhaps a good idea. The first section is very easy going and it's only when you enter the canyon that your legs begin to feel the angle of ascent. Once the climb is done it's downhill for a while but you know that there'll be more climbs ahead. The only people you might see on the course are fishermen by the river to the right of the road. There is also a railway line in the canyon so you'll probably see a very long train pass some time during the marathon, while on the left there are mountains rising steeply.

The two main climbs are at 14 and 21 miles, which are steep and really challenge you but then each is followed by a spot of 'payback' and a downhill section. The climb at 21 miles is the last of the tough bits and lasts for about 2 miles. At that stage in a marathon, it's a severe test of your stamina but if you've paced it right and read the conditions correctly, you'll get through it and enjoy the following downhill bit, which will ensure you finish under the time limit. This course is quite tough but because of the international flavour of the field of runners, the superb scenery, fantastic aid stations providing for all your needs, and a particularly good awards ceremony, where all first-timers receive a special certificate, you'll come away with loads of fond memories and a strong desire to run it the next year.

Peter Graham

The London Marathon

There is no doubt that the London Marathon has had a profound and lasting, positive effect on the people of Britain. It has been perhaps the biggest reason for the increase in the number of people who have taken up running and jogging and as a genuine consequence, has enriched the lives of millions with the many beneficial effects. The needs of all these new runners, has spawned a new industry, precipitating huge advancements in shoe technology and other specialist gear, and that is something that has benefited all of us.

From the moment you fill in the application form for the London Marathon, the excitement begins. You might feel the same nervousness that you experience when writing out a job application or the hopeful expectancy when filling in a lottery ticket, and it certainly focuses your mind on doing it accurately and neatly. It feels special... and it is, because it carries your dreams and desires. Hands up everyone who whispers words of encouragement, (s.w.a.l.k. – athletic variety) before posting it. And how do you react to the December reply? My disappointment on receiving a 'reject' response lasts only a few seconds, knowing that there are so many excellent alternative marathons on or near the same weekend each year. If however, you receive an acceptance reply, do you then perform a little manic dance, break into song and hug the budgie? Or do you perhaps develop an uncontrollable cheesy grin that not only frightens the postman but also alarms everyone in the queue at the bus stop, ensuring you get a double seat all to yourself even if the bus is crowded.

When you visit the exhibition a few days before the marathon you'll hopefully begin to soak up the atmosphere of the occasion because it is an important part of your race preparation and should raise your feel-good factor even higher, which is probably already as high as the 'I can see further than you can' badge on the tricorn hat of Lord Nelson in Trafalgar Square.

On the day of the marathon, there is a sort of serenity throughout Greenwich Park and Blackheath as tens of thousands of runners start to congregate, find a parking spot for their kit bag, join the toilet queue and begin to focus the mind. It is like one enormous family gathering for a huge open-air party, even if it's raining and a black bin liner is the dress code. Some begin jogging nervously yet confidently; they'll stretch, rub Vaseline on to certain parts of their anatomy and work through their personal preparation routine methodically and thoroughly. It might seem that there are millions milling around yet you're still likely to bump into someone you know. The excitement continues to build. Then the 'loads of time' that you thought you had seems to disappear, so you hand in your kitbag to the correct baggage lorry and there are only minutes to go.

Sardines aren't packed as tightly as the runners waiting for the London Marathon to begin, though it is cosy... and when it does begin, from above, it must look like a human telescopic aerial with one end fixed for 30 minutes while the other end stretches out for miles. The shuffle start slowly becomes a jog. Impatient runners explode, weaving in and out from one gap to the next in search of the rhythm that is theirs and the pace that they want. More patient runners just go slow with the flow, savouring and sharing the emotions that are as free flowing as the air they're breathing.

Crowds are cheering loudly, genuinely applauding anyone and everyone while others are looking for dad, auntie or friend. Occasionally they're successful but then the sea surge of runners quickly becomes a blur as thirty thousand rainbows tumultuously bobbing, smiling, chatting, are ripples in a torrent of humanity, honest, caring, fund-raising, eloping with strangers on their own wave crests. Fast, medium and slow pace; old, in-between and young; brave men and brave women conquering the world with – and without – weird, wacky and wonderful costumes. There is no more beautiful moment than now... or is there? The fantasy unfolds gloriously. The spectators – that endless guard of honour – applaud generously, not for a modest 10 minutes, like those recognising orchestral excellence, but for hours and hours for a performance of unparalleled harmony of a physical and mental duet.

Every type of musician will be there to play their part, to blast out their sounds from specially prepared bandstands, from impromptu pavements and from upstairs windows blaring. This scene is unrelenting and ever changing; then just before 7 miles, the famous Cutty Sark is once again engulfed in a sea of runners as the yearly high tide laps against its hull, but beware the shallow waters and the 'bottles of water' reefs that abound throughout the course. They could sink your aspirations.

You'll pass more music, more cheering and more mile markers as they urge you on towards the magnificent Tower Bridge. Can any runner cross this bridge without feeling a sense of... destiny perhaps? I think not.

To enter Cable Street, approach, pass and leave Canary Wharf and the Isle of Dogs, and then join the Embankment is to enter a 10-mile examination of you – an atom-by-atom scrutiny of you. The previous 12 miles were easy, manageable miles, like the first 5 questions in a certain game show quiz, though you will have had help from the audience. But now, the next 10 miles will tell you if your pace in the easy section had been right... or not, your training was adequate... or not, you had read the conditions right... or not, and crucially, you are mentally prepared... or not, because your athletic prowess will now need the support of your mental fortitude as you move towards 20 miles. When you reach it, can you then say to yourself, "Only 10 km to go," and really mean it? If you can, then you'll reach the Embankment at about 23 miles with the mindset to not only survive the last three and a bit miles but to run them with confidence and vigour.

Do the crowds now seem noisier...? Maybe. Will they lift your flagging spirits and tired legs...? Most definitely. Have you saved something for the final miles...? I hope so. Do you get a buzz from each runner that you pass...? If you do, that buzz will empower you with more stamina, enabling you to breeze past 25 miles. Turn away from Westminster Bridge, keep mentally alert and feel invincible as you run triumphantly along Bird Cage Walk and into the Mall. Whether this last bit is agony or ecstasy, stale crumbs or the icing (with a cherry) on the cake, you must finish with head held high because you are a champion, a winner. You are the king (or queen) of all that you behold. Accept your medal with pride as though the Queen herself were presenting it to you. Ride high, but don't stand still. Collect your goodie bag but don't stand still. Haul those weary legs along past the baggage lorries to collect your kitbag but don't stand still, even though every part of your being is screaming for you to stop. This moment is full of beauty too. Live it the full. You will be on a high for the rest of the day, the next day, the day after that and the next, through the physical pain, personal delight and praise from all who know you.

Martin Bulger

The Anglesey Marathon

Only in its third year, Anglesey has got it sorted out down to the last detail. Based at the island's covered showground site, it has something for everyone, from a fun run up to the Marathon. Non-runners are as well provided for as the runners. There's a café; craft, food and charity stalls and a fashion show. Everyone is kept busy! Welsh is very much the first language, and with the spectacular views of the Snowdonia Mountains, it is very easy to imagine that one is abroad.

From the start, the course drops steadily to the coast through small villages, which are anything but small in their support, then climbs back inland to a punishing last few miles! There is also a corporate relay event going on at the same time and at each change-over station there's even more support from incoming and out-going runners, looking considerably perkier than the marathoners! Water, energy drinks, sweets etc are in plentiful supply, cheerfully handed out by the marshals, who seem to be round every corner.

And have they finished with you at the finish? Not likely! A space blanket is wrapped round you, a quality medal hung round your neck and you're off to big plates of pasta, chunks of fruit, cups of tea and lots of friendly praise/sympathy/help and chat. Temporary showers, good and hot are installed and a relaxing massage rounds off the day.

Awards are generous (though the vets categories are in 10-year bands, not 5) and in 2006 were presented by Colin Jackson, who after starting us off, cheerfully spent the entire day chatting, signing autographs, being photographed and generally being a wonderful ambassador for sport. Would I do it again? My entry's already in for next year!!

Jenny Mills

The Venice Marathon

It is officially described as a slightly downhill marathon but some runners see it as simply fast and flat... with a number of annoying corrugations near the end to break your rhythm.

The Marathon begins in Stra, a small town just east of Padova, with the starting line right in front of the magnificent seventeenth century Villa Pisani Mansion. Many will arrive there via courtesy buses, although being crammed in like sardines for the 40 minute drive is not the most relaxing of pre-race preparations and the hectic atmosphere continues with the queuing for toilets and at the baggage lorries, but once you're in your start zone, life becomes easier, allowing you the chance to admire the scenery around you. The route begins by following the Brenta River before wending its way through the beautiful Riviera towns of Fiessa d'Artico, Dolo, Mira and Oriago. Drinks stations are situated every 5 km and the mid-section towns of Malcontenta, Marghera and Mestre seem quickly pulled in and passed, followed by a change of scenery as runners enjoy the greenery of San Giuliano's Park – which was the location of the pre-race Expo and number collection area.

Running by the lagoon gives runners a good view of the Venice skyline with its numerous bell-towers, including the famous one at St Mark's Square. At the 35 km point comes the most arduous part of the course, one that every runner seems to know about before reaching it. It is challenging not for any frightening climb or descent but because it is a dead straight and flat 5 kilometre stretch, just when you don't need it. It's the well-known Ponta della Liberta – the 'Freedom Bridge' that links Venice to the mainland, where psychological, not physical strength is required to get you through. Many runners will take their mind off the drudgery of this part by focusing on the skyline of Venice, the small boats, big ships... in fact anything that will act as a distraction.

In stark contrast, the final 2 km is anything but straight and, with the 14 bridges to cross, anything but flat. Gone is the smooth tarmac surface, replaced instead by cobblestones... and the bridges, conveniently signposted – 'Bridge 13, 12 to go' and so on – are made slightly easier by ramps covering the steps. A sudden left turn brings you to the Grand Canal and a pontoon bridge that takes you across and towards St Mark's Square. Surely the emotional 'high' of the finish of a marathon cannot be higher than that experienced when running through Venice. The tired legs and weary body, with the adrenaline coursing through you, boosted by so much architectural splendour everywhere, the crowds, the gondolas and gondoliers, still more bridges, just one cornetto, give it to me... and the finish banner drawing you on. You long for it to end but at the same time, you want to keep on savouring the beauty of the moment. It was a stunning experience and I rate it as one of my favourite marathons... and most definitely the perfect way to celebrate my 57th birthday.

Karen Bowler

The Isle of Man Marathon

There is a saying on the island which when translated from its Gaelic form is 'tomorrow will do' and this seems to sum up the relaxed easygoing atmosphere that is everywhere on the Island. It is approximately 35 miles long and 14 miles wide and can be reached by flying or ferry. There is so much to see and do, and a real mixture of methods of travel to see all the sights, including horse buses!

There is the Manx Marathon (a real tough nut) at Easter time and this event during August, which is the first of five races in six days as part of the island's Grand Prix road racing series. Many will run all five events and experience the bizarre and conflicting feelings in your legs when instead of taking it easy after a marathon, like any sensible runner would, they are tackling the Peel Hill Race – a very tough 4-mile race up Peel Headland to Corins Foley and back.

The marathon starts close to the Ballacloan Football Stadium in Ramsey and is a two lap course. The first 5 miles are undulating and peak at about 260 feet at the four-mile point and again at 17 miles with the remainder of the course being essentially flat. There are distance markers at every mile and drinks stations every 5 km. The facilities for this event are endless and include free return bus trip between Douglas and Ramsey, medals, goody bags, spot prizes and T-shirts to all finishers. In the stadium there are changing facilities, showers and a huge free buffet. Really, one could not fault the organisation and the checkpoints are friendly and helpful. All marathons are unique, and for a variety of reasons. The Isle of Man event is special because of what the island has to offer to its visitors and the fact that it's part of an amazing week of running when you can clock up 50 miles of competitive (or not) racing, and therefore I can wholeheartedly recommend it, whether you are a relative beginner or 'an old hand'.

Bill Young

The Rottingdean Windmill Marathon

Off-road marathons can be a law unto themselves and cause you to throw away the book of experience entitled 'How to run a marathon' because they're nuts that crack differently. They're unconventional and I'm sure some course organisers take great delight in picking out the highest hills around and linking them with the lowest points. Take the Rottingdean Windmill Marathon for instance, an event that attracts runners, joggers and walkers, offering them either 8, 15 or 26.2 challenging miles on an often baking hot day in July.

It begins in a narrow, wooded, yet built-up valley and the course descends erratically towards the coast east of Brighton, passing the windmill very soon after the start but even so, only once your sprightly opening gambol has been reduced to a mountain goat stagger. Then the first of the dead flat stretches, at about 2 km, takes you along the coastal Under Cliff path to Saltdean but don't be fooled by it or the three other similar easy bits... the ones that traverse the Ouse Valley to Itford Hill at 8 miles, the A27 corridor to Mount Caburn at 12 miles and the levels just to the south of Lewes to Kingston Hill at 19 miles... But the hills in between... oh, the hills in between... they rise and descend so sharply that the grazing sheep will pause and look at you and applaud your brave efforts. It's the steep-up, steep-down and dead flat profile that destroys the likelihood of a runner settling into any sort of rhythm that they'd normally adopt in an ordinary road marathon and has so far prevented anyone from breaking 3 hours.

Like many cross-country marathons, you'll be given a sheet or three of detailed route instructions and even though the course is clearly way-marked, inevitably there'll be pauses to check you're on the right path or occasions when you stop, unable to see the next route arrow (a case of runners' blindness). Negotiating the variety of running surfaces that the course offers will conspire to impede your progress, as will the stiles, gates, sheep, cattle-grids, pubs, ditches and rutted ankle-breaker field crossings, all wildly wrapped in so much natural beauty.

It is tougher than the **Beachy Head Marathon** (looking at people's finishing times I'd say about 10 per cent tougher) not just because of the high temperatures that tend to occur but also as a result of its unusual profile. The **Rottingdean Windmill Marathon** is long-established (over 25 years), well-organised and a must for off-road fans and any pussy cats who want to eat flint.

Martin Bulger

Chapter 4

Contributors' Own Stories

Jenny Cobby – Henfield Joggers

I used to be the typical couch potato until a dramatic life-changing moment in 1995.

I'd smoked since the age of 15 and done very little in the way of exercise but suddenly, for no apparent reason, I gave up smoking and made a conscious decision to do something about my life. I was 45 and decided to take up running. Sneaking out after dark for an anonymous lone jog, or walk and jog was not for me so I joined Steyning AC, a small, friendly club near Brighton. I could manage only 400 metres in those early days yet even doing such short distances, I still experienced the famous feel-good factor and I was hooked. After entering several local West Sussex Fun Run League races, then a Ladies race in London and a number of half marathons in Hampshire and Sussex, I began to dream of completing the **London Marathon** but realised that a lot more extra training was needed. I had often watched the TV coverage of the event and thought that it must be a wonderful challenge to complete it, but never thought that one day my dream would actually come true and it certainly didn't enter my head that I would enjoy it so much that it would become the first of many marathons.

The support and encouragement that I received from my running colleagues at Steyning AC was superb, and crucial to my preparation for that first marathon. What better way is there for a runner to celebrate their fiftieth year than to run a marathon. I finished it in just over 5 hours and enjoyed it so much that I travelled over to America to run the New York marathon later that year, completing it also in just over 5 hours.

My 'runners high' was sky high as I ran over the finishing line of both events and I felt so pleased at being able to complete two marathons in the same year.

Running is my number one pastime and I race most weekends somewhere in the south of England. At my speed of running, I am never going to win a race or be anywhere near the front, so why do I run? Quite simply, it's for the pure enjoyment of being outside, running through the countryside or along the seafront, the sense of well-being from exercising, hearing the cheers from the spectators and other runners, and the buzz that you get when you cross the finishing line. I've now done other capital city marathons, such as **Paris** and **Dublin**, and several off-road marathons, including **The Seven Sisters**, yet those same feelings are there whether it's a marathon or 10 km, 30,000 or just a hundred runners.

I plan to take part in the 2008 **London Marathon**, which will be my sixtieth year but before then, I have my sights set on the **Washington Marine Corps Marathon** in October.

When will I stop? I can't ever imagine giving up running so I intend to carry on jogging, visiting new places and running their marathons, soaking up the atmosphere, waving at the crowds and thoroughly enjoying myself.

Considering how unfit and unhealthy I was in my younger days, I have become very proud of the cabinet at home that holds all my medals, trophies and other mementoes. My motto is: Change your life for the better. Take up running and get rid of all the stress of life. Keep on running.

******

Brian Winn – Hailsham Harriers

My first 26-miler was the inaugural **Worthing Marathon** which, although it was back in 1983, I do remember well. The course, round the roads of the town and surrounding area, is spirit-level flat but for a very brief climb up and over a railway bridge in the final half km.

I started the race with Keith Emerson, famous for his lead role in the pop group, Emerson, Lake and Palmer, and an experienced runner. We ran together but I became envious that he was getting a lot of support from the spectators and I was getting none. We stayed side by side until I 'hit the wall' at about 20 miles. I told him to push on as I was getting slower and slower. Passing through an area known as Sompting a woman on the pavement shouted out, "come on little 'un." I looked behind me and saw no other runners around at the time so I assumed she must have been directing this unflattering remark at me. However, it woke me up from the stupor that I had fallen into and I found a 'second wind' that kept me going, finishing in 3 hours 30 minutes.

It then became my ambition to break 3 hours but it took nine more years of trying before I actually achieved it, at the flat Windsor to Chiswick **Polytechnic Marathon**. I sent out my application to run the race well in advance of the event but throughout the week leading up to race day I tried to pass my entry to someone else in my club as I was feeling unwell. Taking on a marathon is not something one should do without adequate preparation and certainly not when you're feeling under the weather but the day of the race dawned and no one seemed eager to take my place so, with a cavalier attitude and a large helping of 'mind over matter', I decided to go for it.

One of the golden rules of marathon running is to never wear anything that you haven't got used to and worn in but in the euphoria of it all, I forgot it. I was wearing a newly purchased jock strap and after a half an hour felt a rubbing between my legs and after a few more miles I was aware of chafing. Luckily, I thought, I spotted someone from the Honda Goldwing Club of Great Britain on his motorcycle cruising past me and I shouted, "Vaseline, Vaseline." However, it was as if I was speaking a foreign language as he looked back at me in a most uncomprehending way. This unsuccessful form of communication was repeated time and time again with other bikers as they rode up and down the course. I can only conclude these chaps, who were meant to be looking after the runners' needs, were unable to hear anything underneath their crash helmets. Nevertheless, the discomfort I felt in the nether regions made me forget the fatigue I must have been feeling in other parts of my body, or perhaps I was just desperate to finish as soon as possible to end the pain. Whatever the reason, I pressed on and finished in 2 hours 57 minutes achieving my ambition (but red raw in the groin area.)

The decision taken before a marathon of what to wear on the day of the race is obviously quite crucial but caution is thrown to the winds when one is foolish enough to contemplate running it in fancy dress costume. Running 26 miles is challenging enough without the extra burden of wearing something silly. Under normal conditions, every ounce of your being is stretched to the limit when you run a marathon. If it's hot, you make adjustments to your approach. You wear lightweight gear, moderate your pace and drink plenty, wear a cap and perhaps sunglasses too, and you survive the experience. I have worn a gorilla suit twice in the **London Marathon** for two reasons. One, to raise money for charity and two, to hopefully get seen on TV. The first time I donned the outfit I discovered that I had two other gorillas to contend with so I made certain I was the first one home. The second time I wore the disguise I found I was the only one stupid enough. On both occasions I lost half a stone in weight and presumably the other gorillas must have suffered to a similar extent. However, on completing the marathon in just over 4 hours, the immediate wish after proceeding through the finish is to rip off the sweat soaked costume. What I hadn't bargained for was a zip jamming, forcing me to catch the underground train still dressed in a ridiculous outfit which I couldn't escape from. That year I had arranged to meet up with some friends in a nearby public house, which would have been within walking distance, had I been suitably attired but the short underground train journey was the slightly less embarrassing option in the circumstances.

Running marathons abroad adds an extra dimension to the enjoyment factor and I have great memories of the **New York**, **Brussels**, **Paris** and **Berlin Marathons**, the last of these being the first time the organisers could take the race into East Berlin.

When I ran **New York**, I shared a room with another runner and on the day before the race we were invited to participate in what the organisers described as a breakfast run. We both took part but my room mate stubbed his foot badly and could hardly walk afterwards so back at the hotel, with him horizontal and by propping his leg up with the throbbing toe uppermost, I wrapped it in a plastic carrier bag full of ice cubes. He stayed in that position for virtually the rest of the day but it seemed to work because the following morning he was lining up with me at the start line. Amazingly, he finished in just over 3 hours with me a further 18 minutes behind.

A flat section of the **Paris Marathon** takes the runners alongside the River Seine and I particularly remember enjoying the view of Notre Dame Cathedral but then being distracted by a very attractive lady dressed in a Wonder Woman costume who was overtaking me. My lasting memory of the **Brussels Marathon** is the cobblestones at the finish, not a pleasant surface to run over after the best part of 3 hours.

The question often put to me by non-runners is "why do you run marathons?"

My reply points towards Greek mythology, the challenge of running a classic Olympic distance and the satisfaction of raising money for charity. I enjoy running whatever the distance and having seen two photos of me, one before a marathon and one after, it is quite clear from my body language and general demeanour the toll that it takes on the body. Having said that, there are runners who positively fizz after a marathon and whose 'runner's high' keeps them in orbit for weeks.

******

Peter Taylor – Sittingbourne Striders

I took up running as a direct result of commenting on the unflattering profiles of some of the runners that I saw in a Rotary Club half marathon that I helped to organise many years ago. "If they could do it, so could I," I said recklessly. Some would describe that remark as an own goal, while others might call it a lucky break... or destiny. However you perceive it, it opened the door ... and I walked in. The following year in that half marathon I ran 2:12, yet while I was still enjoying that moment of achievement, I began to feel the need to break 2 hours, so I did it again the next year and recorded a tantalising 2:00:30. I was hooked and entered the Faversham half marathon a few months later and knocked a further 4 minutes off my PB. Inevitably, the full marathon beckoned and after 3 attempts to gain a place, I ran the 1992 **London Marathon**. I have since run the London nine more times.

******

Richard Honeyman – Seaford Striders

I'd seen the **London Marathon** on TV many times but it was in 2003 when I decided to travel to London to watch the event 'live' that I began to wonder if I could actually run myself. I saw Paula Radcliffe and couldn't believe the speed she was doing and it was while I was walking from Canary Wharf to the Embankment Tube Station and soaking up the fantastic atmosphere of the event that I made up my mind to take up running. I joined the Seaford Striders later that year as an absolute beginner and the fear that I had about running clubs, that one had to be fit and athletic before joining, was unfounded. I did have doubts and felt a bit self-conscious on that first evening thinking "everyone's looking at me." They with their sleek appearance and smart gear and me with... well, I must have stood out like a sore thumb. The truth was they were just ordinary people, a mixture of all ages and abilities who just happened to share a love of running.

I enjoyed those first months of running, going from a combination of walking and jogging to nine-minute miling, culminating in my first race, at the Chichester 10 km in February 2004, clocking 51 minutes (just over 8 minutes a mile.) The following month I stepped up the distance significantly and took part in the popular Hastings Half Marathon. Noted for its steady and seemingly endless climb from the seafront to the eight-mile point, it descends (perhaps too steeply) to sea level and a dead flat 3-mile dash to the finish. A most challenging course but definitely enjoyable... and for me, a time of just over 2 hours. It was there that the atmosphere generated by the huge crowds and the camaraderie of the runners convinced me, if I needed any more convincing, that running was for me.

With each race, my confidence grew, my speed increased and I felt much stronger. As a result, the floodgates opened in 2005 and I entered twenty six events, including most of the races in the Sussex Road Racing Grand Prix series. One of those was the Worthing 20, which I did in 3 hours 13 minutes, and having done it, I was certain that I could run a marathon. I chose the **Dublin Marathon** in October and devised a training plan that would increase my mileage and use other shorter races as preparation, mostly in Sussex.

I've been to Dublin before and love its unique character and, like London, it has a pre-race expo which is an ideal opportunity to meet and mix with other runners and feel the atmosphere building up. Race day arrived and I was up at 5:30 am as were many other people in the hotel, to have an early breakfast. I returned to my room and, as I donned my running gear that I'd laid out meticulously the night before, it began to feel different. Although it was my first marathon, I had done loads of other smaller races but I began to sense something special. Perhaps it was just nervousness, excitement and uncertainty of the unknown. I turned on the TV to catch the local weather report and uninspiringly it said "very changeable" which I feared would mean a mixture of light, medium and heavy rain. It started raining shortly after 8 am and was still pouring down when the marathon began at 9. Sensibly many runners wore bin bags to keep dry but it didn't really work and I was quite soaked when the race got under way but I didn't mind... I was going to enjoy the day. It took 10 minutes to cross the start line and even then, the pace was slow but that actually helped me to settle into my own pace and not dash off like a reckless loony. The route passed Trinity College, crossed the River Liffey then headed to the north of the city and I found myself chatting to other runners. "Hi there, buddy," came a voice from an American runner... then I was running alongside a local girl who was also doing her first marathon and who felt obliged to apologise for the atrocious weather. Another lady next to her was on her eighty-seventh marathon. I am sure that the camaraderie in a race increases proportionally with the length of the event. In a marathon thousands of people, strangers, are thrown together yet very quickly share their thoughts and experiences with other runners as if they were close friends. One might pass along a pavement packed with shoppers and not utter a word to anyone but here, on the streets of Dublin, there were friendly, spontaneous conversations everywhere.

Luckily, the rain eased off after the first hour as I passed through Phoenix Park so I ripped off the bin bag and felt like superman. Then, for the next two hours it was showery but I was really enjoying the race. However I had no idea where I was in the outer suburbs. The crowds were huge all along the course and in some neighbourhoods people were wearing leprechaun costumes, at least I assume they were costumes! It was fantastic.

I passed the halfway stage at 2 hours 5 minutes feeling strong and on course to finish but then suddenly the race changed to being serious as the atmosphere became noticeably quieter and everyone began to concentrate. Perhaps it was reality kicking in... another 13 miles to run and the first half had been flattish but there were two hills to come. However, I ran them both which boosted my confidence – for a while – and had no problems until the 24-mile drinks station when I slowed to a crawl and stopped to have a drink. My leg muscles began to feel very tight and it became a mind battle. I wasn't comfortable walking, I wanted to run but that was also painful. It was the psychological versus the physical. The battle raged for two miles but when I realised I was near the city centre I could feel my spirit lifting. There was a downhill stretch then I lapped Trinity College again and turned right into the finishing straight. It was amazing that at this point my speed increased quite dramatically and I ran strongly to the finish but then it seemed a bit surreal. The noise and heady atmosphere was so different from other races that I don't think I could take it all in but what really mattered was... I had run my first marathon!

I enjoyed receiving my medal and goody bag and was extremely impressed by the efficiency of the marshals and other officials who seemed to control everything like a well-organised machine. As for me, I was meant to be ecstatic but in reality I was so relieved to finish with no injuries that I went back to the hotel, showered and watched a film on TV. It was my wife's birthday so that evening we went out for a double-celebration meal and some Guinness.

My first marathon was a very powerful experience despite my subdued feelings at the finish so I decided to run another one, following the same format of tying it in with a weekend break in a city I'd never visited before and chose the **Amsterdam Marathon**. Interestingly, when I started running again after Dublin it felt weird.

My legs seemed to have lost the knowledge or will to run and I felt again as if everyone was watching me but thankfully, entering the Brighton 10 km three weeks later helped me to recover both mentally and physically, and allowed me to once again run with confidence.

I had the whole summer to prepare for Amsterdam, using a number of much shorter competitive races and the Henfield and Windsor half marathons. I found that they helped me to further develop my knowledge of how to run races, which is something that doing just ordinary training doesn't really achieve. For instance, how to run the different stages of a race, whatever the distance and how to gain maximum help from the crowds and fellow runners. My target for Amsterdam was to break 4 hours or at least to set a PB as my training had gone well, though with not as much speed work as I would have liked.

I'll never know whether my failure to achieve it was due to insufficient quality training or because of a cock-up with the baggage system at Gatwick which resulted in my kitbag not arriving until after the marathon had taken place. The holidaymaker's nightmare had struck and although I was able to purchase a complete set of new kit at the Exhibition, the psychological damage of it all was not so easily overcome, not least the fact that I didn't sleep on the Saturday night for worrying about what had happened.

That apart, it was almost ideal weather conditions, the course was flat and the race started and finished in the impressive Olympic Stadium. At the mass start, being surrounded by foreigners (obviously) it felt strange not being able to chat and share your thoughts with anyone, something that normally helps to settle any pre-race nervousness but when the marathon began, it didn't seem to matter because of the fascinating city streets, the canal system and running through Vondel Park, which seemed to be a most enjoyable distraction. Although I haven't done many marathons, I have taken part in many other races and can appreciate the added dimension that running abroad gives to a race, particularly marathons. The low point of the race came around the 20-mile mark when my stomach began complaining about something I had eaten and my hamstrings weren't happy about things either but then the route approached the historic city centre and the crowd support became greater and it seemed to give me a lift until I was running at the pace I'd been hoping to do. I was only 3 minutes outside of my Dublin time but I wasn't too disappointed, because despite the setback of the missing luggage, it was the atmosphere of Amsterdam and the camaraderie that seemed to know no international boundaries, that enabled me to enjoy the race and I can't wait to run another one.

******

Julia Armstrong – Brighton & Hove City AC

I run marathons because I was born to run. The moment I could walk I ran and have been running ever since. I run marathons because I love the journey. For me, the best bit of a holiday is often the time spent getting to the destination. I love airports and train stations. I love the 'hands free' freedom of travelling, of journeying unencumbered. I love driving through Europe, to arrive feeling richer for the journeying, the miles unfolding, the peace descending.

I have found through making the journey my goal, that my life has become a rich tapestry of experiences and that through following the road less travelled, I have learnt about me and, within that discovery, my understanding of the human condition has deepened and grown.

I am a seeker. It has always been thus. I came here and have been seeking understanding all my life and have discovered that within the truthfulness of competition on foot, just one step after the other, nowhere to hide, just me and the ground beneath and the next step ahead, I am finding my own truth.

I have run all my life, in a circle, round and round, running towards and running away from at times, my destiny. Each time I circle around again I have stripped off another layer, I am that much nearer myself.

And why marathons specifically? Because there is mystery within the marathon footrace. I believe that the training for a marathon gives gifts that no one realises until they commit to their marathon path. Even to run a reasonable marathon takes a deeper commitment to self than one would know. The distance is 'too far' for the body and so within the decision to run a marathon lies a touch of madness and of course, the truth is that once we acknowledge our madness, we are on the road to freedom and unique individual expression. A marathon has within its hands the gift of each person's journey, if they dare. Running a marathon is as simple as one foot in front of the other and as complex as any human being. This is the joy for me. During training and running marathons I am in touch with myself and I know who I am in a way that nothing else can achieve. I am at ease. I am invincible. I am a child of nature, at one with the universe whether battling into an icy wind or flowing along on a summer's day. The marathon has given me a deep trust of myself and my innate strength. It has given me the knowledge that I will survive anything. In running and finishing a marathon I think that it has been possible for me to glimpse my soul, revealing many of its facets and to see the flame that burns bright within, and to know even if for only a split second, that innate talents lie within me and potential beyond anything I ever dreamed. These secrets revealed, even fleetingly, have meant that I have continued to seek all my life for what I know lies within us all: truth and beauty and clarity, strength and wisdom, and love. The marathon reveals to us the human spirit at its best. Aspiration meets inspiration, striving for excellence, to become more than we already are and so change the world with each step we take.

******

Roger Ockenden – Arena 80

I started running in 1980 at the age of 32. Until then I had played cricket, football, squash, badminton, tennis, table tennis, ten-pin bowling and a variety of other sports, all to a reasonably good standard and on a regular basis. I also enjoyed walking and gardening so I regarded myself as very active and extremely fit. In the first few months of my running I only did races and training runs up to 10 miles. However, the TV images of the 1981 **London Marathon** inspired me to increase my training and prepare for a marathon. During the 1980s I ran ten marathons, including the 1986 **London Marathon**, all of the **Worthing Marathons** and one in Hampshire.

The others were events organised by the Sussex LDWA (Long Distance Walkers Association). In those days I was capable of running 36 minutes for 10 km, just over the hour for 10 miles and around 1:21 for the half marathon. With these times, running a marathon in under 3 hours (a target for so many club runners) should have been feasible but for some inexplicable reason, the best time I achieved was only 3:16. It didn't seem to matter what the weather conditions were, whether I had trained well or under trained, I always had a really bad time at the 18 to 20 mile mark resulting in the last quarter of the marathon being pure torture with only willpower getting me to the finishing line. Strangely, whenever I did a walking marathon I never had the same problem.

I even tried different approaches for my last marathons – slower pace for the first 13 miles, increasing my food and drink intake prior to the race but all to no avail. I can still recall the pain after completing my first marathon. My legs had such bad cramp that I was unable to drive myself home afterwards. For anyone who is about to run a marathon, don't be put off by my experiences as I'm sure they are quite rare. By the early 1990s and after 20 marathons I realised that 26.2 miles was not for me and I have not run one since.

However, I have just completed 25 years of running and have taken part in over 2000 races. I still get a 'runners high' after each race and training run. It's just a shame that I never felt like that after finishing any of the marathons I ran.

******

John Gill – Haywards Heath Harriers

I believe that the marathon has a very distinctive aura and mystique, and considering the large number of runners who are piling up a cricket score of marathons, it must be deduced that they are addictive, not to the detriment of life, I hasten to add, but for their life-changing effects and the way they enrich people's lives. Why should this be? Is it perhaps the straightforward physical challenge that any marathon race issues to all competitors? Or is it the fact that the very distance takes any runner into areas of extreme mental endurance? Maybe it's the incredible camaraderie that has developed within the marathon fraternity? Or is it that those who have run a marathon or two believe they have found Shangri-la? Who knows!

My own fascination began well over 50 years ago although my personal involvement did not finally start until 1982. Almost immediately, I became hooked on marathon running, mostly off road because I found them to be far more satisfying than pounding the tarmac for 26 miles.

The reason why I run marathons began for me long ago in the early 1950s when as a youngster I delighted in being able to read the sports pages in the daily papers and one of the first people to capture my imagination was Jim Peters. He had, I discovered much later, been a finalist in the 10,000 metres at the London Olympics in 1948, finishing in ninth place. Soon afterwards, he moved up to the marathon and in his debut was the first Brit to go under 2 hours 30 minutes. He went on over a period of some four years to set four world records and in the process was the first man to break 2:20. He was the world record holder for 6 years and all this was achieved wearing plimsolls. I wonder how many people could do that these days? Sadly, it was his two dramatic failures as much as these great achievements that really fired my ambition to run a marathon one day.

At the Helsinki Olympics in 1952 he was the hot favourite and was running shoulder to shoulder with the legendary Czech athlete Emil Zatopek. It is claimed by some that at the half-way point Zatopek said, "Hey Jim, are we going fast enough?" Peters replied "No," and immediately increased his pace, only to suffer severe cramp in both calves and have no option but to drop out. Two years later at the Vancouver Commonwealth Games he entered the stadium more than 20 minutes ahead of the second placed runner, who had all but given up because he did not realise he was in a medal position. Unfortunately, Peters was in a severely dehydrated state and, in perhaps the most heart-rending spectacle in athletics history, desperately tried to complete the final 200 yards, only to fall repeatedly and, for the final time, just a few yards short of the finishing line. It is known now that the support for the runners on that day fell a long way short of what would be required today and cost our man a gold medal that should have been his.

At the time I was too young to take up the challenge and for many years I was engrossed in rugby and cricket so gave little serious thought to this old ambition. However, it began to resurface following the 1964 Tokyo Olympics when the full-length film of the event was on general release. I had two reasons to see the film – my obvious interest in the sport plus the fact that I knew the man who did the actual commentary. Those who saw the film may recall that it finished with the marathon and a very moving sequence involving, I think, the runner from Tanzania who became injured and extremely tired but refused to give up as he believed that it would demean his country if he dropped out. He was so far behind the other athletes that some of the day's events had finished and the crowds had begun to disperse. Nonetheless, the Japanese kept all the finishing arrangements in place until he finally completed the course, but in some distress.

My ambition then came closer to the surface through the 1970s when I read a series of articles in the *Sunday Observer* by Chris Brasher. He wrote very graphically about endurance events and the stories surrounding the exploits of people such as Joss Nayler, Kenny Stuart and Billy Bland amongst others. His writing also covered marathons in some detail and by the time he announced the first **London Marathon** I was totally determined to do one. By 1980 I had retired from rugby and cricket, largely because I could no longer afford them. I now had a young family and was also being severely affected by the crippling interest rate on mortgages at the time. Even so, I had become less than happy about my lack of fitness and had already started to go out on short runs with some regularity. So inevitably, I applied for the first **London Marathon**. Equally inevitably, I was rejected but having put in a fair amount of training, I was determined not to waste it so I looked around for another, and giving myself an additional 6 months of training, I entered the **Southampton Marathon**. The day came round all too quickly but the ambition was thwarted when my car blew a top hose on the Chichester bypass on the journey there and by the time I had got it fixed, I was 20 miles from the start but with only 15 minutes to get there.

Rather than being put off by the experience it actually renewed my commitment, and having been given a couple of copies of *Running Magazine*, I looked through the first one, decided to enter the **Masters**

and Maidens Marathon at Guildford, and sent off my entry form. A few days later I opened the second magazine to see an editorial note saying that the **Masters and Maidens** race was fully subscribed. Was I fated never to run a marathon? This time I checked the magazine for other reasonably local runs and sent off entries for the **Three Forts** and **Farnham Castle Marathons**. A couple of weeks later I received numbers for both events as well as the **Masters and Maidens**, together with an apology for the erroneous editorial. So, at last, I was in business... but perhaps too much business!

My debut was thus the **Three Forts Marathon**, just outside Brighton, subtitled the 'Tough One' and with over 3000 feet of ascent and descent on its original course this was a fairly good description. The late June day was beautiful, hot and sunny. Just what is needed for a debut marathon! It all went very well as I enjoyed some parts of the South Downs that were new to me – going over Chanctonbury Ring, Cissbury Ring and the Devil's Dyke and I still remember the euphoric feeling crossing the finishing line in 3 hours 57 minutes. I also well remember having to go down the stairs backwards the next morning but I stayed on cloud nine all week having fulfilled my ambition 30 years after that Helsinki Olympiad.

The **Masters and Maidens** (meaning in this case, veterans and debutants) therefore became my first road marathon and a time of 3:15:58 was pretty satisfying, one which I improved on just a whisker to 3:15:15 a month later at **Farnham**. Marathons then became a fairly regular feature in my life and the next ambition was, as you would expect, to break 3 hours. The race I targeted for this was the **Worthing** event in April 1984 and, perhaps rather stupidly, I entered the **Guildford City** race, due to take place in March, as my final serious training run before the big attempt. I fully intended it, my sixth marathon, to be a solid training run, nothing more. The weather at Guildford started cold and dry but threatening trouble and, sure enough, before the end of the first of the two laps the heavens opened. It didn't just rain... it was absolute stair rods of torrential downpour. Not only did the runners get very wet and bitterly cold but also some of the course became flooded. On lap two, runners had to negotiate sandbags and ankle deep water. However, there was little choice really but to keep on running or freeze. In spite of the problems – or because of them – the finishing clock showed 2:59. I was so surprised and delighted at this achievement that it seemed to ease the pain of hands too cold to undo shoe laces or remove soaking kit. Eventually, I did get back to my car where the elation quickly vanished on seeing the ground on which all the cars were parked waterlogged, resulting in everyone having to wait their turn for a tractor to tow them out of the mess. The next month, **Worthing** was far less traumatic but only a scant two seconds faster. There were another four 'sub threes' and my benchmark for a potential marathon best, a half in 1:19 and a 20-miler in 2:07 suggested I was capable of about 2:45 to 2:50. Unfortunately, these indicators are not the same as actually doing it and the best I managed was only 2:57. Now, 20 years on, running under three hours for a marathon is beyond me but at least I can still perform, albeit at a slower pace.

The fascination with endurance athletics had begun to take hold by this time and a number of ultra distance events beckoned. The 40-mile Mendip Trail Race, the similar distance Otter High peak race in Derbyshire and the Fat Ass 54 along the North Downs were all hugely enjoyable events, but my favourite, however, has to be the South Downs 80 mile race, which I completed 9 times, achieving a best time of 11 hours 51 minutes which I rate as my best ever performance over any distance. These races all seemed to produce a wonderful level of camaraderie and support not always so evident in the town 10 km races we all know so well. I have to say that for me the off road races are far more memorable than those around the streets of towns and cities. If you have not done so already, try the **Beachy Head** (previously the **Sevens Sisters**) **Marathon**, a marvellous event complete with superb scenery, including maybe 20 or so climbs, musical support from a Scots piper and brass band, very supportive marshals and a fearsome descent over the last 200 metres to the finishing line.

I was eventually accepted for the **London Marathon** on four occasions and once managed to slip under 3 hours to record a course PB of 2:59. This was when my best time entitled me to a 'fast for age' number and a place in a very civilised starting enclosure just outside the gates at Greenwich Park. It took only 30 seconds to cross the starting line, a real luxury in such a huge field of runners and I think it was on this day that I experienced my personal saddest moment in a marathon. At about 12 miles I suddenly realised that I was running alongside a very pretty young lady in basque, stockings and suspenders but try as I might I could not keep up with her. Although I have this and other fond memories of London I have always found the smaller fields and better scenery of provincial events far more appealing and they do give you the satisfaction of finishing (with a bit of luck) in the first hundred and not something in the region of fifteen-thousandth. Indeed, I once finished a marathon in fifth place, which sounds impressive until I confess that there were only 48 runners in the race! One of my most memorable marathons was the 1989 **Seven Sisters** when the wind blew up most alarmingly in the later stages of the race. On the most exposed parts of the course, along the coastal path, by Belle Tout and Beachy Head, around the 22-25 mile point, when legs were weary from all the unrelenting hills, runners were being blown over or even lifted off their feet and at Birling Gap car windscreens were blown in. It got so dangerous that as soon as the leading runners reported the problems, the course was re-routed inland, away from the cliff edge as a safety measure. Runners in Sussex can still be heard asking "were you there the day of the big wind on the Seven Sisters?" I also ran this event when there were snowdrifts of over six feet on top of the Downs and can recall with a wry smile the incredibly deep mud of the **Chanctonbury Marathon** that strangely seemed to get deeper each year... and the unsettling experience of reaching checkpoints before they had opened on the **Rottingdean Windmill** and **Three Forts Marathons**.

On the whole, I have been lucky enough not to experience any major problems in marathons although it is inevitable that you get tired as the event unfolds, and sore feet and aching legs have to be expected but I have only once had a problem with the infamous 'wall'. This was at the **Poole Marathon** when the start was delayed for 45 minutes because part of the course, the swing bridge, had to be 'swung' to let out all the private pleasure boats while the tide was high. This was fateful for the athletes because shortly after this late start the morning mist dispersed and the sun came out. Up until then I had been determined to set a new PB and was well set at the halfway point in 1:23 but in the next few miles the heat began to do its worst and I subsided to a disappointing second half of 1:52 and a moderate 3:15 finish.

For me, one of the ongoing fascinations of the marathon is the way runners react after each race. Obviously, some are more tired than others, leaving some distinctly more jovial than their peers as they all try to regain their general equilibrium after the finish. So many will be heard regaling anyone in earshot with how difficult the race was... and how they did not see how they were ever going to finish... and that they will never again be daft enough to enter a marathon. But you can bet your boots that a few minutes later these same people will be seen picking up a handful of race entry forms for the coming months and hobbling triumphantly back to their car with a bizarre smirk on their face. This makes me think that there must be a memory-dulling drug in the adrenaline that drives a marathon runner to complete the distance or in the lactic acid that builds up in their muscles... or brain.

******

John Errey – Seaford Striders

As a member of St John Ambulance in Crowborough, East Sussex, I joined my colleagues on duty in Greenwich one cold April morning, following an invitation to our division to help cover the **London Marathon**.

We had been promised an exciting, interesting and long day. This proved to be right. We were issued with our jar of Vaseline and then allocated a stretch of the route close to our First Aid Post. Once the elite runners had passed through we had a little wait before the steady stream of runners became a flowing colourful river of fun runners, some wearing costumes attracting attention for themselves or their chosen charity. Gradually, it became a trickle of people going by just enjoying themselves. I came away from the duty thinking "I must do that some time."

I did the same duty the following year and afterwards had the same thought. I tried, unsuccessfully, to enter a couple of times but eventually I did get lucky and began my training by running each weekend.

The race in April 2001 was an incredible experience. My wife and daughters met me at various points along the route, a route that was full of people and entertainment. Musicians of all types outside churches, on traffic islands and pub balconies encouraged us on our way. Making their way to the finish my family saw me at Westminster but from then on I was 'gone' just following the road, carried along by the sea of cheering crowds. Then Buckingham Palace came into view and I could see the finish halfway up the Mall. All exhaustion disappeared and I floated up the Mall to the finishing line. I had done it!

I found my way to the pub where St John Ambulance (my charity) had set up a reception for their runners and was glad to sit down. Unfortunately, when I was asked to go back outside for a photo session I could barely move. Somehow I managed to stagger out on painful legs but elated that I had run my first marathon in 5 hours and 7 minutes.

Two years later I ran the 2003 **London Marathon**, again raising money for St John Ambulance but virtually gave up running after that. However, in 2004 while chatting to a neighbour, Gloria Woodford, she asked if I was still running. When I owned up to having hung up my trainers, she persuaded me to give it another try and join her on Wednesday evenings running with members of the Seaford Striders Running Club. I did just that and found myself entering a host of races. This focused my attention on marathons again and I targeted London 2005. Although I was not accepted, I did receive a guaranteed place for the **Edinburgh Marathon** in June 2005 and I have since run four more marathons including a number overseas.

******

Joyce Smith – Hastings Runners

The feeling of being unfit can either lead to a passive acceptance of one's own deterioration or prompt a reaction against it. Walk to the corner shop instead of drive to the supermarket out of town, buy a bike or take up swimming... but in my case, my husband, Ron, and I decided to join the local sports centre and try a weight training course, followed by a warm-down swim. We thoroughly enjoyed our new found interest and went on to do circuit training and aerobics. Although we'd never run before, we also decided to add jogging to our list of activities and very soon our week consisted of three weight training sessions for Ron, with three circuit training sessions for me, both of us swimming afterwards, three bouts of aerobics followed by a short run and a longer run on the Sunday. In no time at all we felt super fit… and ready for anything. So, we both entered the 1988 Hastings half Marathon and I remember the sense of achievement when we crossed the finishing line and received our medal. I remember too, thinking it was so easy that I could have run twice the distance with no problem.

My first attempt to gain a place in the **London Marathon** was not successful although I did persist in trying to get an entry other than through the ballot and with just two months before the 1989 event I received an acceptance. I had kept up my jogging after the 'Hastings' but had to increase my training quite considerably to be in a position to take on the challenge. Eventually the great day arrived and I lined up near the back of the heaving mass of runners who filled Greenwich Park. It took about 20 minutes to pass through the park gates but I didn't mind because I just wanted to enjoy the whole event, as I assumed it would be a one-off experience. I was totally captivated by the sights and sounds from beginning to end, the different bands playing and the ghetto blasters blaring out all manner of music from upstairs windows and balconies, the friendly chatter between runners and the humorous and encouraging banter with the unbelievable crowds who were eager to play their part. It was fantastic. In fact, I was so bewitched by the whole electric atmosphere that it wasn't until I had reached the 15-mile point that I realised there were mile markers with blue and white balloons arched over the road. I had been enjoying every minute so much that I just hadn't noticed them.

Once I realised how far I'd run and how good I was feeling, I just began to picture myself collecting the medal at the finish. It also helped seeing my family at four or five different spots around the route and then I remember cruising down Bird Cage Walk and into the Mall on cloud nine and finishing the race feeling absolutely chuffed with myself. I don't think I stopped smiling from the moment the start gun went off until I went to bed that night. My time of 4:40 didn't seem a particularly good time to me but, I'd done it. I'd run a marathon.

Next morning was a different matter though, my legs ached and I felt drained, but after a couple of weeks I began to think that, with a better training schedule, now that I knew what it was all about, I could do better. So, when the entry forms came out for the 1990 **London Marathon** I entered again. This time I got in under my own steam as a 'good for your age' runner (well, I was now 48). So again training began in earnest with a few changes and thankfully, a bit longer to get miles under my belt. I did more longer runs, including running the Hastings half marathon route both ways straight off. If you know the course and think the route is hard, try also running it in reverse!

I was now a member of Hastings Runners so it was nice to be able to start the race with runners I knew rather than being on my own as I was the year before. However, it wasn't long before I was running on my own again as my fellow Hastings Runners were more experienced and faster than I was but that didn't spoil my day. It was terrific and I was feeling good and running better than the previous year and certain I could do a faster time. I even noticed the mile markers this time. Once the race had settled down my strategy was to pick a runner in front of me and to gradually dig deep and catch them up, have a quick chat to catch my breath then press on to the next targeted runner. Each runner I pulled in and overtook gave me enough buzz to catch the next one and so on. You get such a good feeling when you catch someone up and pass them and I'm sure it was this tactic that helped me to achieve a better time; in fact I clocked 3:58, an improvement of 42 minutes.

I'd begun to really get the marathon bug now, and in every race I entered, whatever the distance, I became more competitive and, because I continued to better my times, I decided to enter the **London** again. When the forms were out I entered knowing I would probably get in again due to my age and time from the previous year.

My preparation for this, my third marathon, was more organised and again was done with the dedicated help of my husband Ron, my daughter's friend Michelle, Nigel Baker and other Hastings runners and included long training runs up to about 25 miles, more varied routes and even some speed sessions back and forth along Hastings seafront. All this extra more purposeful running meant I was feeling that I had timed my training just right and I would 'peak' on the great day.

I was determined not to get too 'carried away' at the start though and didn't really settle into a stride pattern that suited me until I passed the 5-mile point, but by the time I ran past the Cutty Sark I was feeling on top of the world and running well. I was lucky to spot Ron at 8 miles because I was way ahead of my schedule, a plan that he had so painstakingly worked out the night before the race. Again I picked out runners in front of me to catch up and overtake, which helped me particularly round the tough parts of the course. The exuberant London crowds once again worked their magic by encouraging runners, lifting you when you were low but it does make you wonder just how they manage to keep up their amazing vocal support for what must be hours on end. And if your name or club name is on your running vest, they cheer you personally, like they know you and keep you feeling on top of the world all the way to the finish. I did slow up a bit during the second half of the race but still managed to finish in 3:45 (the target I had set myself), reducing my PB by 13 minutes this time.

I did run the **London Marathon** the following year, clocking 4:03, a time less than I'd hoped for due to a back problem that reared its ugly head during the race. That was my fourth and last marathon but I still have very fond and emotional memories of marathon running that, I know, will stay with me for ever.

******

John McFarlane

I initially started running as a way of keeping fit for my main activity which, in the early 80s, was hill walking and mountaineering. I was entering my middle to late 30s and like anyone, my youthful fitness was becoming a thing of the past. I knew that I would have to work at it and do some sort of training. I played kick-about football with the children but realised that this was not enough.

In June of 1984 a friend of mine, Bill Turner, announced that he was doing the Sawbridgeworth Fun Run in Hertfordshire and would I like to join him. I said "yes" and the following weekend saw me run the 10-mile course, wearing plimsoll-type shoes and football shorts. I recorded a time of 81 minutes and was left with two souvenirs, a chafed inner thigh and a black toenail, but more importantly, I had enjoyed the event.

I carried on jogging in the evenings and at weekends, doing short runs and a few weeks later bought some proper shorts and a pair of running shoes (Hi Tec Silver Shadow). Somewhere along the line I decided to run the local marathon, probably because one or two people I knew had already entered. It was due to take place that October at **Harlow** in Essex (an event that is sadly now defunct) and I embarked on a training programme of my own design, which was something of a 'crash course' as it was now late July and the marathon was only three months away. Unfortunately, from early August onwards I had recurring niggles with my right knee, causing a significant disruption to my training schedule but I did manage one long run of 15 miles and a few more between 10 and 12 miles.

By late October the knee problem had returned but I was fortunate that through my (then) employment I was able to obtain free physio treatment and in the week leading up to the race I had three sessions of ultrasound which seemed to 'normalise' the knee. The day of the marathon dawned with me feeling quietly confident but with no clear idea of what time I was capable of. At the start I set off and got into a reasonable rhythm fairly quickly and reached the half way stage thinking "this isn't too bad." The course itself was unremarkable and not exceptionally hilly. The weather was cloudy but dry and I was enjoying it, especially as my knee was behaving. This good feeling did not last however, and between 17 and 18 miles I started to feel drained and very tired. Shortly afterwards I was unable to run all the time and was reduced to run, walk, run, walk. The last five miles were tough and I eventually crossed the finishing line in a time of 4:38. I had experienced the 'sting in the tail' and although I was a bit disappointed with my time I was pleased to have finished and glad to have a medal to prove it.

A few days later I decided I wanted my marathon time to be 3 hours something and resolved that I would continue to run until I achieved a sub-4 hour time. My training, such as it was, continued and I heard in December that my entry to **London Marathon** the following April had been accepted. In early April I had a recurrence of the knee problem so I quickly got more ultrasound treatment and lined up on the 21st April 1985 for the start of the London. Again things seemed to go quite well up until mile 18 when the pain kicked in once more. I didn't slow down quite as much this time and finished agonisingly close to my target by recording a time of 4:02. I did raise cash for Muscular Dystrophy with this event which gave a purpose to it all and made up for having missed my target so narrowly.

My next attempt at the sub-4 was at the very beautiful **Loch Rannoch Marathon** in Scotland in June of that year. This course was possibly the most scenic I have ever run and it's a great pity that it has also ceased to exist. I improved my time ever so slightly but was still tantalisingly outside my target at 4:01.

That October saw me line up once again for the **Harlow Marathon** but since Loch Rannoch my mileage had been particularly uneven, recording as little as 6 miles one week whilst my greatest weekly mileage was a 'massive' 30 miles. My unscientific training schedule did not worry me and I was confident of a sub-4 hour time. Once again I got to about 17 or 18 miles and felt rough. Whether it was experience of this painful situation or just plain obstinacy, I slowed down even less this time and with just a mile to go I had nearly 10 minutes left to 'crack it'. Realising the chance to achieve my ambition, I ran the last mile in 7½ minutes and finished in 3:58. I was elated. Those two simple, unbelievably important minutes made me feel so happy. Illogical – yes, even silly – but there you are, that's the magic of the marathon. I carried on running more marathons, getting to the point where a sub-4 was nothing out of the norm for me. Between late 1988 and early 1989 I ran five marathons in five different continents in five consecutive months, starting in **New York** and finishing in **Sydney**. I used it as a fund-raiser for an Oxfam project raising £5000 towards the construction of a child care centre in

India. I wrote to the Guinness Book of Records who confirmed that it was a record but was too specialised for inclusion in the famous book. In one 12-month period I ran thirty-six marathons and got to the point where I did little or no training between marathons. Running one almost every weekend seemed to suit me and I seldom got injuries and was able to recover from each event very quickly.

I carried on running marathons until 1993 when I was made redundant from my job and having to concentrate on building a new career, my marathon running ceased for a while, although I did keep up the jogging. Whilst on a hiking trip to Switzerland in September 2003 a chance meeting with some runners who had just run the **Jungfrau Marathon** rekindled my interest so I stepped up my training just enough to be able to run the **Miami Marathon** the following February, clocking just over 5 hours... I was back on the treadmill!

In running all these marathons I have been able to see much of the world and at the same time, raise plenty of cash for causes that have appealed to me. I intend to carry on and may even reduce my PB even further when I retire and have time to train properly.

The marathon distance is special and a real test, a human challenge like no other. When you reach the finish you have proved your persistence and ruggedness. Few things in life are as satisfying but why we run them is difficult to analyse. After so many marathons I ought to know but to be honest, it is still a mystery.

******

Peter Hooper – Eastleigh RC

The thing they don't warn you about when first running a marathon is the sheer addictiveness of running 26.2 miles. Certainly, when I started back in 1999, I thought that just the one would be enough – been there, done that – but here I am, ten marathons down and an hour and forty minutes faster, with the magic sub-three tantalisingly, frustratingly close. Part of the addiction is of course the dopamine-induced high, finishing a race strongly, outsprinting someone younger to the line, setting a PB, doing well for the club or just for me, all contribute to the obsession of doing better. Part of it is adding new races to the diary – the **New Forest, Paris, Berlin, Boston, Chicago, New York, LA, Sydney** are all on the wish list. Unfortunately, most of them are likely to remain there. Part of me thought I'd call it a day after ten, seeing as it's a nice round number... except that I've only done **London** four times and really ought to do it a fifth time... but then I'd be finishing on eleven marathons... which is a real nothingy kind of number, so then it will have to be fifteen... and then...

It's not just the dopamine fixation, of course or the slightly worrying fixation on nice neat numbers. A huge element is the knock-on effect of training for this ultimate athletic challenge. No other distance has quite the pain, the endurance, the speed, the 'just beyond the wall' agony. Getting into shape to run – no, to race – 26.2 miles sets you up for a whole new level of fitness. Pre-1999 I'd always enjoyed hill walking and assumed a day's walk of about 25 miles was about my limit. Suddenly (well actually, I mean suddenly after a year's training) tough walks became a lot easier. Silly distances, over 30 miles in a day became do-able and eminently justifiable as excellent endurance training for the next marathon. The Welsh 3000's was a turning point – fifteen 3000ft mountains spread over 33 miles of Snowdonia, completed in 17 hours with two marathon-fit friends... and hill walking was swapped for trail running and trail running led to fell-running... and fell running opened up a whole new game. Covering over 40 miles a day, seeing huge tracts of country that others rarely get into. Starting mid-summer epics at 2:30 in the morning and only needing a head torch for the first half hour, picking a route through an ancient hill fort with only a beam of light and the ghosts for company. Brilliant!

Chris, a friend who got me started on the road to hill-junkie, has got it worse than me. He's graduated from marathons to **Marathon Des Sables**, Jordan Desert Cup, Tour de Mont Blanc, Alaskan and Andean adventures and now Primal Quest. Google the names and you'll find some great events and great websites. Me, I'm happy staying with the South Downs Way, the Across Wales Walk, the Old County Tops, the Three Peaks (the proper Yorkshire one, not the tourist trail one) the Lakeland 3000's and shorter, more brutal events like the Grizzly and the Meon Valley Plod. However, despite our diverging geographies, Chris and I share the same holy grail – the Bob Graham Round. Read 'Feet in the clouds' by Richard Asquith and you'll understand why. A tale of magnificent obsession. 72 miles, 42 Lakeland mountains, 23 hours 59 minutes 59 seconds if it's going to count. 24 hours and one second... and it's a meaningless failure. The trouble is, if we do it... no, when we do it, I know what will happen. 72 miles...? OK, why not a hundred...? And I'll do a hundred. And Chris will do something else... the Death Valley Race probably, not for the bragging rights but just because he can... and because it's there.

So we come full circle. We ran trails to be better marathon runners. Now we run marathons to be better mountain runners. But still nothing hurts more or pushes us more beyond our limits than those 'beyond the wall' miles in a marathon. Get past that and anything is achievable... break through that barrier and there are no harder hurdles. That's the magic of 26.2.

******

John Leather

Ever since I was very young I have always run, not walked. The doctor said to my mother, so I've been told, "he will run before he can walk."

In some ways I have been very lucky as I have built my running around this natural God-given ability. Unfortunately, it developed into an obsession to cover an illness enabling me to cope with life. This has meant that I have not enjoyed something for which I was naturally gifted. I 'conned' myself that I was enjoying it. Believe me, this does not work as eventually, sometime during your life, everything catches up with you!

I am a strong disciplinarian, with the ability to go through barrier after barrier and can push myself far beyond what most people would only dream of. Nature has a way of warning you that it is time to stop, that mind and body have had enough. So beware of the consequences that may occur if you try to defy the warning! Adrenaline can be a very powerful drug allowing you to carry on when the whole body is screaming out for you to stop. My illness of anorexia didn't help as I was often running on an empty tank. It just doesn't work.

I feel it is important, whether running marathons, track races, cross-country, ultra distances or fell running, inspired perhaps by magazine articles, television programmes, watching others or feeling the need or desire to get fit, that your aim should be enjoyment, rather than, as in my case, an obsessional 'chore'. We have enough things in life that are necessary and may go against the grain without turning running into one.

At long last, after several serious injuries and getting older, with help I am slowly coming to terms with the personality problem which led to anorexia so that I can now enjoy my natural gift.

To every negative side, there's a positive one because it has meant that in some ways I am physically very fit. I am below my recommended weight for my height, meaning I carry less baggage at every step and I really do admire those people who I see running to lose weight, having difficulty in breathing yet who persist and conquer running.

Because of my love of nature and the countryside it has meant that I have concentrated on long distance, off-road events. I do not like road running, in fact, I have only ever run one road marathon and that was enough. I much prefer it when you can experience the soft moss underfoot, tufty grass, muddy paths, grassy paths, rocky paths, crossing streams and small rivers, even stiles, although I do find them a bit of a nuisance as they break one's rhythm. Kissing gates are better. I have seen beauty everywhere – flowers, trees, mountains, rivers and valleys, felt the warmth of the sun on my back and the wind in my face and, to a far lesser extent, the enjoyment of rain, snow and hail. All this comes as standard in the huge variety of off-road events that can be found in the British Isles.

Although this book is meant primarily to tell the story of why people take up running and then move on to and stay with marathons, I think it is necessary to pass on some of the knowledge that I have gained through my experience of running. Whether any would-be runners take up what I say is up to them. Each runner is unique, an individual, who will hear and read all sorts of advice but must decide what to take on board and what to discard. I believe that trainers are the most important item in the runner's kit bag. There are plenty of specialist sports shops who will help you get the pair that suits you, whether you are flat-footed or high-arch, pronator or supinator, light or heavy runners, on-road or off-road, you name it and there'll be a shoe for you. I use Hi-Tec Silver Shadows, a no-nonsense trainer with a shock-absorbing insole and that suits me. Buy and wear the gear to suit the type of running you're going to do and make comfort and practicability the main factors, not necessarily something that looks good and trendy. I have a thermal Helly Hansen base layer, a mid layer and a rip stop nylon waterproof top and Ron Hill tracksters. Being a mountain and hill runner, I do carry rip stop over-trousers on most events as it can be many degrees lower up on the mountains and hills compared with down in the valleys.

Obviously, you must have an aim, a motivation, to take up running and then you should experiment with various events to find out which you enjoy most. Many would suggest that variety keeps the legs and mind focused and happy. Mix too, the way you tackle an event. You don't have to run each race as if you intend setting a PB. That's a quick way to injury and disappointment. I know of some runners who will jog a marathon as training for a 10 km race as well as racing a 10 km in preparation for a marathon.

Above all, enjoy your running and use it positively to help you through life's ups and downs. I write this particular point from the experience of my own life when running was a chore, not an enjoyment.

******

David Beattie – Crawley AC

After the initial question, "How many days (or miles) do you run a week?" non-running folk often ask, "What do you think about while you are running?"

I find this just about impossible to give a direct answer, though some of my most creative ideas occur on a training run, but the reasons why marathons and ultra distance running have become part of my life can be seen through the highs and lows that I've experienced in my training and racing.

As a youngster I lived on a council estate on the outskirts of Seaford, East Sussex, and the plethora of footpaths nearby gave me easy access to Seaford Head, Cuckmere Haven and the Seven Sisters Cliffs. My pals and I would often explore the countryside, and follow on foot as the horses and hounds chased foxes through Friston Forest and across the open hills around East Dean and Jevington. The hunts often seemed rather unsuccessful and we would chuckle as a fox walked across the track within ten yards of us, while the pursuers were heading along the skyline in another direction.

We would also pursue fire engines on our bikes (chimney fires were common but more spectacular were haystacks on sun-dried fields) and we competed to be the first to arrive at the scene. Another favourite pastime was to ride down High-and-Over hill towards Alfriston. This is a very steep narrow road with a severely devastating Z-bend at the bottom – the first one to apply their brakes was a chicken! All this activity and more was what we did all the time. Football matches on the recreation ground, with jumpers as goalposts, would last all day with only a brief pause for lunch before resuming with the score in the twenties and perhaps 17 players on each side!

My childhood was unbelievably energetic and so school cross-country running came naturally to me. It was seen as a mere extension of my out-of-school pastimes, but on the track I lacked the speed for the shorter events. I gravitated to the 2-miles (the longest race on the inter-school programme then) and I competed for Brighton AC in cross-country races, road relays and at 3 miles and 6 miles on the track before hanging up my spikes and turning to football (and beer) for the next ten years.

Aged 29, I started running with Crawley AC. I had lost a lot of stamina but with training it gradually returned. For a couple of seasons, track and cross-country races sufficed then I was attracted to longer events. Before my first marathon, I read that an over-distance run was recommended, so I entered the South London Harriers 30-miles road race as training for the **Harlow Marathon**. I set off with Tony Lintern, a club-mate, and running at a cautious pace we thoroughly enjoyed the experience, overtaking several who had started far more quickly. Many marathons followed, and the most satisfying were those where the pace judgement was right for the course and the conditions on the day. I love the more challenging marathons, like the **Isle of Wight**, rather than the fast flat courses. I have also noticed that the tougher events seem to attract a fair number of 'characters' who make the sport so endearing. Many spring to mind, for example, Mark Pickard, who would regularly run marathons back to back on Saturday and Sunday, or Paul Taylor of Woodstock Harriers, who interpreted the rule that 'vests must be worn' all too literally – Paul's vest usually contained more holes than material, and he sported an amazing selection of colourful socks and shorts (on closer inspection the latter proved to be swimwear or boxers).

It was Paul Taylor who turned to me as we were in the first ten miles of the old Woodford to Southend 40-miler, and said of the runners scattered down the road ahead, "They'll all come back at 30." Paul was right, and therein lies one of the attractions of ultra distance racing – the race goes to the one who judges his effort to perfection rather than the fastest on paper.

Another great thing about our sport is that the longer the distance, the more sporting are the participants. Each runner is striving to perform to his best level, but genuinely wishes his fellow runners all the luck they deserve. If someone passes me in the closing stages of a marathon or ultra, they deserve a word of praise for a well-judged race. Conversely, a runner who has 'gone for it' and blown up deserves encouragement for gutting it out to the finish.

Back to the characters. Paul Woolgar of Crawley loved to wear fancy dress in races, despite which he raced at a high level. On one of the hottest days of the year, he wore a dragon costume for a 40-mile road race, and he once ran from London to Brighton wearing an exotic South American bird costume. Poor Sam Lambourne of Brighton must have thought he was hallucinating, each time he turned round to see his pursuer. A track 40-mile race on May Day saw Paul turn out dressed as a maypole – I was unfortunately whipped about the face by his coloured streamers – and to add insult to injury, he won the race.

One of the pleasures of long distance running is the opportunity to explore the countryside on foot, either alone or with training companions. After a week of M25 commuting, I enjoy the early

Saturday morning ramble with my club mate, Wally Hill – we refer to it as our weekly 'therapy run' when we can get things off our chest and put the world to rights.

Holidays often provide a chance of really challenging terrain, and some of my happiest memories are of running for hours along the rugged coastline of North Cornwall, with the sea crashing into the granite cliffs and rocks far below, and each climb resulting in yet another magnificent view. The Lake District, North Wales and both Devon coastlines all hold special memories, with a huge collection of creased and soiled Ordnance Survey maps a testament to the training in all weathers.

Some long races offer the chance to make a weekend of it – the Two Bridges in Scotland and the Dartmoor Discovery spring to mind. Often, the post-race disco and numerous beers made an overnight camp an experience to remember. One Dartmoor Discovery a few years back, four Crawley men crammed into one tent, but the chap furthest from the door (who had drunk the most) kept treading on everybody else in his haste to answer the call of nature. I woke at one point to see a pointed snout push under the tent flap, and leapt out to see a fox making off with our cornflakes.

Some runs remain in the memory for different reasons. Last year my wife and I were staying in the Brecon Beacons and I ventured up on a cold clear February day, with a woolly hat, gloves, thermals etc, and a rucksack full of emergency rations. I had picked up a route description from the local holiday park and followed its clear instructions until I arrived at a spectacular waterfall, then followed a rough track which soon disappeared under snow. The going became trickier, with the route description warning of numerous sink holes to avoid with care. After turning the page to read "from now on, skilled work with map and compass is essential," I discovered that I had set out with neither map nor compass – unbelievable!

Luckily, just before the sun disappeared behind the clouds, I managed to "guesstimate" in which direction I should be heading. My luck was really in that day – I 'navigated' to the exact spot where a Wellington bomber had crashed in November 1944. Standing amid the few weather-bleached fragments that remained of the aircraft, with only the noise of the wind for company, I reflected on the young men

– younger than my own two sons – who had perished for their country that night.

The rest of the run, apart from falling into a bog, was fairly uneventful. I found some old mining tramways mentioned in the guide and ended with a spectacular descent in the last few miles. Since then, when venturing into rougher country, I have been very careful to pack map and compass.

Talking of map and compass reminds me of my pal, Jim Parker, who I introduced to running over 25 years ago in the Gower – the deal was that I would go rock climbing if he would go running. With my fear of heights, the first phrase I learned was "tight rope!" as Jim hauled me past a tricky section. He introduced me to Mountain marathons – the **Saunders** and the **Lowe Alpine**. They were fun in their way but I lacked Jim's ability to stand and look over a precipice and announce calmly that he could see an easy way down. I still can't believe how he talked me into descending that stone chute off Crinkle Crags. I was usually exhausted but happy after these weekends – I believe that challenges such as these events are great for building one's mental toughness and self-sufficiency.

The parallel with marathon and ultra distance running is that at some stage everyone hits a rough patch. In a mountain marathon it may be a poor route choice or sheer bad luck with start times and the weather. In road races it is simpler. Those who have prepared well and race wisely, get what they deserve. Those who may not have prepared so well, or have misjudged the pace, can still achieve deep satisfaction from performing to the best of their ability on the day.

I guess that is the attraction of our sport. Even when the odds are stacked against you, if you struggle through the bad patches, you can look back on the event and grin. As Sri Chinmoy says, "the memory of your heroic effort will survive even when your success or failure are long forgotten."

******

Linda Jennings – Seaford Striders

I hold the BBC responsible for involving me in marathon running. The very first televised **London Marathon** inspired me with a burning desire to participate in the event and the programme's signature tune has never failed to send shivers down my spine or set my pulse racing. However, the odds of becoming a marathon runner were stacked against me as I was born with a collapsed lung and whilst still a baby I contracted whooping cough. During my teenage years I smoked but in 1977, after many unsuccessful attempts, I finally succeeded in kicking the habit, only to contract pneumonia and pleurisy a year later. Before leaving school in 1969 I was in the cross-country team but then did little in the way of exercise for a very long time. In 1989 and 1990 I competed in a Scouting Association team hiking event along the South Downs Way, gaining second and first place respectively. I enjoyed the outdoor life that Scouting had to offer and considered myself reasonably fit. When I saw octogenarian Jenni Wood-Allen run a marathon I was really inspired, believing if someone twice my age could run a marathon then I most certainly could.

After years of trying I was finally rewarded with a place in the 1990 **London Marathon**. My father had died of cancer a few years previously and so I decided to raise money to buy invaluable equipment for the Eastbourne branch of Macmillan Nurses and also make a contribution towards a new van for my Scout Group.

I religiously followed the marathon training guide and covered many solitary miles along country lanes surrounding my home. The weather that spring seemed particularly unkind for although I love running in the rain, I really didn't enjoy running against gale force winds.

My first marathon day eventually dawned. I drove up to London Bridge Station, parked outside and caught the train to Greenwich. I was amazed at the vast number of runners crowding onto the train. Everyone was so friendly. Strangers actually spoke to each other, exchanging experiences, offering advice, eagerly anticipating the day ahead, all full of hope and with dreams to fulfil. It was my first experience of the camaraderie amongst runners and I was a complete novice as far as marathon running was concerned. Although training had gone well, I still didn't know whether I was capable of completing a marathon. That morning I was bubbling with suppressed excitement, full of anticipation and very apprehensive but gaining confidence from listening to the tales of other runners. I was in my element. On that occasion, the finish was on Westminster Bridge and as I came past Big Ben and under the time clock straddling the finish line I was bursting with emotion. I had achieved my dream. Only a runner completing their first marathon will understand the euphoria I felt at having put my body through such a testing experience and won through. I could take on the world and win. An element of sadness crept in, reminding me that my father wasn't actually there to share it with me. Shortly afterwards, an old family friend whilst congratulating me on my achievement, reduced me to tears saying how proud he would have been of my efforts. After that first marathon I unfortunately had an injury, then lacked the incentive to run alone and really needed a specific goal for motivation.

After my second **London Marathon** in 1994, I decided to join a local running club and not allow all the training to go to waste. I haven't looked back since. The support I found from being with friends all sharing the same passion was invaluable. I was well and truly smitten by the running bug and have derived enormous benefits from it. I also acquired a great deal of self-confidence which helped in my everyday life. When I first joined Seaford Striders I competed in many races and to my amazement, actually won the occasional trophy. Nowadays, due to my limited finances I tend to select races more carefully, choosing ones I believe will give me the most pleasure. Running has helped me through some difficult times. Some might say it was responsible for my marriage ending in divorce but it helped me overcome the stress of the break-up, the menopause and the possible threat of thinning bones without medical intervention and I derive such immense pleasure from running along the South Downs.

In 1997 I helped provide back-up for a friend who was participating in the 'South Downs Way 80' and that provided more inspiration for me to take on longer distances. Back in 1990, I had only intended to run the one marathon just to prove to myself that anything is possible when you set your mind to it, but somehow, along the way, I became addicted. I have a friend who claims to get a buzz from moving house every few years. I prefer a less expensive option and get my kicks from running.

I love running; it gives me such a buzz. I'm not fast but I have the stamina which allows me to run the marathon distance and sometimes beat colleagues who excel in the shorter, faster races. I adore being in the countryside, wind, rain or shine. I particularly enjoy the early mornings, especially in the spring and summer time. The air is cool, fresh, and the day promises to develop into something special. I like to watch the world waking up, lights coming on in homes, people going to work or walking the dog. I run along the cliff-top and rabbits scatter before me, or up on the Downs where, as the day warms up, skylarks are bursting with song. I love observing the seasonal changes in the countryside especially as spring arrives. After the dull, depressing winter months, it gives one hope for better things in the blossoming year ahead. Each week new flowers bloom in the hedgerows, first the catkins and snowdrops, then violets and primroses, followed by the snowy blackthorn blossom before the bright leaves emerge from their buds, covering trees in a fresh green haze. It is wonderful. The sounds of birdsong fill the air and silvery cobwebs shimmer with the early morning dew while I run along the riverbank with wreaths of mist gently drifting above the fields. Pairs of swans gliding peacefully upstream, swallows and house martins swooping and diving over the water catching insects or gathering mud for their nests are just a few examples of Nature's beauty. One evening, a startled badger shot out from the hedge before me and I chased it along the footpath until it disappeared into the bushes. On another afternoon there was the scream of a rabbit as it was caught by a stoat.

Above all is the most wonderful scenery and wide open skies. The undulating South Downs speckled with sheep, woodland nestling in the hollows and a whole network of chalky tracks and footpaths to tempt you to explore. My favourite spot between Bo-Peep and Firle Beacon fills me with an immense felling of freedom. I feel on top of the world as I look south towards the glistening sea or inland at Mount Caburn, where I played as a child, and then gaze on the vast patchwork of fields stretching far away to the Downs in the north.

Marathon running is, for me, the thrill of nature combined with the freedom of the outdoors and the excitement of a physical challenge. They are the reasons for running but probably why I don't break any records and why I prefer off-road marathons. I don't feel quite so conspicuous if I take 5 or 6 hours to jog around the course, and I can enjoy the companionship of fellow runners and the wonderful countryside that Southern England has to offer – Chanctonbury Ring, Duncton, The Seven Sisters, Salisbury Plain or the New Forest are just some of the attractions to savour.

The only road marathons that I can honestly say I enjoy are the **London** and the **New Forest**. They are the only marathons where I actually watch the time clock and attempt to complete the course in a respectable time. The appeal of London lies in the cheering spectators who urge struggling runners on, and the camaraderie amongst runners. Whilst running, complete strangers chat, offering words of encouragement to each other. The **New Forest** offers wonderful scenery along with a challenging course and I have run my second fastest marathon there.

Each marathon is different but all provide a challenge, which when met, gives immense pleasure and a sense of achievement. As I grow older I am slowing down and feeling more aches and pains, but I can't begin to imagine a time when I cannot run or escape into the countryside.

******

Chapter 5

The Lighter Side

The reasons that we give for having a bad run or race are numerous and sometimes voluminous. Some are genuine but it is quite obvious that others are pure fantasy, in fact downright lies. So, in an effort to clean up our sport I have itemised the top twenty-six reasons/excuses (that's one for each mile of a marathon) that will be acceptable and given each of them a number. All we have to do now is to quote the number(s) then sit back and listen to the respectful commiserations. Won't that save a lot of time and be a lot more honest?

<u>REASONS</u>

1   Arrival at the finishing line was delayed due to leaves on the pavement.
2   Got lost because the satellite-tracking device fitted to my undergarment malfunctioned.
3   Drank too much beer/wine last night.
4   Dog bit me.
5   Ran slower while having to remove ill-fitting and uncomfortable underwear.
6   Lost a shoe in the muddy puddle from hell. You should have seen the mud. It must have had the suction power of a hundred octopuses. I only just managed to pull myself out.
7   Tripped over a pair of discarded underpants.
8   Bit dog.
9   Badly sprained – a) Achilles. b) calf. c) soleus. d) quads. e) muscle corpuscles. f) hams. g) gluteus maximus. h) back. i) arm. j) leg. k) brain. l) shoulder. m) upper body. n) lower body.

10   Exhausted after party game went badly wrong (variation of no 11)
11   Ran with injured elbow, caused by falling off a gerbil.
12   Not enough beer/wine last night.
13   Stress at work.
14   There was a cloudburst leading to a series of flash floods. This caused the local river to rise so high that it spilled onto the footpath that I was on, forcing me to seek refuge in a pub.
15   Met an old friend who forced me to follow him into a pub.
16   I stopped to give directions to an alien.
17   I chased a mugger who was attacking an old lady. I now have a £1000 fine or 3 months in jail for causing him distress.
18   I was impeded by a gale force 17 wind in my face. It was so strong that I couldn't see where I was going... took a wrong turning and ended up in a pub.
19   I made a citizen's arrest of an old lady who had refused to hand over her bag to a mugger.
20   I swallowed a fly.
21   I stopped to think of an excuse.
22   I stopped when I saw a three-legged tortoise with a limp, who obviously needed an ankle to cry on. You see, he'd been badly let down by the organiser of a bungee jump and was nursing a bruised bum. To make matters worse, he'd had to jog all the way round someone lying on the pavement who'd just... (see number 7) and if that wasn't bad enough, he'd also been molested by a short-sighted traffic warden who had mistaken him for one of Auntie Maggie's home-made crusty meat pies. Anyway, we jogged together for about 3 metres then I nipped into a pub (see number 3) while he sped up the High Street to the Clothier & Pet Shop to buy a shell suit. The big question is, do you think that this tortoise taught us to repeat ourselves?

23 Pulled a hamstring arm-wrestling a tortoise.
24 I kept having to stop for a wee. I don't know why.
25 Ate too many crusty meat pies.
26 All of the above.

Marathon review

The New World (Wild West) Marathon

In 1506, just fourteen years after he had discovered America, Christopher Columbus decided to organise a marathon. The cowboys liked the idea but the Indians had reservations. However, many tribes of Native Americans did take part, with all finishers winning an engraved wagon wheel. The event was won by Big Chief Running Sioux and the first lady home was a timid woman known as shy Anne. There was a particularly big cheer when Davy Crockett arrived at the finishing line, looking funny with a patch he had on his levis and there, sat on a chair, a key figure keeping an eye on his digital sun dial, was Caseyo Jones, recording all the finishing times. After 4 hours and 56 minutes came the last of the Mohicans. A grey-haired old man called Bill won the vets prize but was later disqualified when it was realised that he had covered part of the route on his pet buffalo. The team prize went to the Mayflower Striders, while the award for the first overseas competitor went to Fileus Fogg, who was wearing the original 'I ran the world' T-shirt. The trophy for the best young athlete went to Billy the Kid.

The route had been clearly marked with arrows but they were stolen shortly after the race and later used in an attack on a stagecoach. In the St John Ambulance wigwam, the duty officer (an Indian warrior known as Germolino) had only three problems to deal with – a runner who tripped over a piece of pipe, another who tripped over a pipe of peace and an Indian who had a paleface... caused by a severe attack of the wild Bill Hiccups.

In addition to Sioux and Mohicans, did you detect the three other tribes hidden within this story?

The Bethlehem Marathon (a Christmas story)

It was a clear starlit, night as competitors continued to pour into town for the first ever Bethlehem Marathon. There was an air of excitement as if people sensed something special was due to happen. Would a world record be set or would every runner achieve a PB or maybe, an unknown person would arrive and become world famous?

The arrival of a large team from the Shepherds Jogging Club seemed to raise expectations and they were joined by a host of angelic-looking athletes sporting natty and aerodynamic winged T-shirts. They were full of praise for the event organiser and sportingly wished all the runners good luck and calm weather.

The hotels filled quickly and the bars and restaurants were buzzing with talk about the laser light show that seemed to shine like the brightest star they'd ever seen. Joseph Carpenter from Nazareth AC who was travelling to Bethlehem for the marathon with his pregnant wife, Mary, arrived very late due to the wrong type of sand on the camel trail and although they had a booking at the Bethlehem Barn Youth Hostel, their room had been taken by a group of unattached runners, so they had to kip down in the cycle shed at the back.

Anyway, just as Joseph was pinning his race number on his vest and laying out his kit and trainers for the race, would you believe it, there and then, right between a state-of-the-art hi-tech tri bike and a baker's bread-delivery bike, Mary went into labour.

Quietly, the ever-resourceful Joseph unbolted two panniers from a couple of bikes and stretched out his long rucksack across them, making a trendy hammock (an idea he had cribbed from someone).

Before you could say, "New Balance shoes are the best," the baby was born.

"Shall we call him Moses, after Moses Kiptanui, the Kenyan 10,000m runner," asked Joseph, "or Brendan after that nice Mr Foster or perhaps Harvey, after my favourite tipple?"

Mary looked at Joseph as if to say. "Der...!!! No, he looks like a Christian, yes, I think Christian suits him. And anyway, have you noticed the halo above his head? Did you put it there?"

"Not me, Cherub," replied Joseph.

Just then, three runners from the far East (The Goodwin Sands Running Club) called Caspar Ying, Melchior Yang and Billthazor Young arrived bearing gifts. They were known as the three Ys men and they brought a gold carton of 6 energy drinks, a pair of Frankie's socks and a tube of aromatic Vaseline rub.

The young Christian did grow up to become world famous and even now, his miraculous achievements are still talked about.

Little known facts about marathon running.

+   150 years ago Queen Victoria led the way in fashion and sophistication by sporting a carved ivory and lace fan. 1000 ladies were offered the chance to win a similar fan by running from Admiralty Arch up the Mall to Buckingham Palace. The winner of London's first marathon fan run received the prize.

+   Al Jolson, the famous American singer of the 1920s was also an ultra marathon runner. This fact came to light in his most famous song, when he sang "I'd run a million miles for one of your smiles..."

+   In the 1930s top South African athlete Johannes Coleman trained for marathons by stealing ostrich eggs. It wasn't the protein in the eggs that made him a fast athlete but being chased by the ostriches after stealing them.

+   For those wishing to enter the Tokulu Marathon, be warned. It may be cancelled following the very poor response to the 2005 event. Despite finishing in the spectacular Mowam Eddow Stadium, the marathon attracted only a single athlete, the Polynesian champion, Wayne Toomo. This resulted in the following news headline in the Tokulu Gazette – **One man, Wayne Toomo went to Mowam Eddow.**

+   Proverbs 4, verses 26-27 states, Ponder the path of thy foot, and let all thy ways be established. Turn not to the right hand nor to the left. Remove thy foot from evil... In other words, beware of hills, avoid boggy terrain, don't get lost and you may stay injury-free.

+   A Chinese proverb – A journey of a thousand miles begins with a single step.

+   William Tell, the well-known fourteen century Swiss biathlete (archery and marathon running) used the contents of his lunch as target practice. He would put his cheese sandwich, penguin, apple and can of cola on a fence and shoot arrows at them. One day someone ran off with his apple so he shot at the thief .

+   In Greek mythology, Achilles was the perfect marathon runner. He was strong, fast and courageous but his invincibility as an athlete came to an end when running in a Swiss marathon. He was hit in the heel by an arrow shot by a local archer while eating an apple at a checkpoint.

+   Fred, a marathon runner from Tunbridge Wells in Kent, often went up in a hot air balloon with his neighbour, Jim, as part of his mind preparation before running an important marathon. Fred and Jim had been friends for years and years until they fell out.

+   Veteran Molly Fudge (aged 95) puts her continued love of running marathons down to her healthy life style. She is a real stickler for cleanliness when it comes to her diet and even washes her tea bags in boiling hot water before using them.

The Baker's Two Dozen (and a bap) Marathon

This tough course is not suited to the loafers of the world but those with inbread instincts, who can rise to the occasion, slice through all the hazards and who doughnut back away from a challenge.

Sandwiched between the beautiful South Downs and the flantastic English Channel, the route climbs quickly on to the ridge, and kneads lots of stamina. It's no bun run, I can tell you. Brighton and Hovis in the distance as you pace tree-lined paths (or is that pastry-lined paths?) towards the first checkpoint. With more hills to climb before you reach the next checkpoint you'll realise that it's going to be no piece of cake so you'll be glad to arrive at the drinks station for refreshments (not a wholemeal). The route then heads yeast until it reaches the river which you have to croiss an' turn right to make your way to the coast. It will almost certainly be a warm sunny day so it is advisable to wear a bum bag (or an even smaller bag-ette) to carry a hat and some sunglasses. If you've been pudding in some hot-weather training and you're wearing bran-new trainers, you'll probably enjoy the section of the route that takes you along the seafront just as much as the hilly tart of the course. I have to admit that I prefer the grassy footpaths that are everywhere on the Downs. Every flower that I see, even a plain flour makes me marvel at the beauty of nature. It's not pie in the sky to say that I wish every marathon was as picturesque as this one.

After checkpoint 3 the winding course climbs again but the route is very clearly marked. You'd have to be a real muffin to go wrong here, although it did happen once to the ladies course record holder, Patti Surrey. She got in a real flap. Jack, her husband, fortunately realised their error and they returned to the right path. Beyond the half way checkpoint a pizza the course runs through a wood before dropping down to sea level again for a few miles. For the next section of the route you'll knead to roll up your sleeves (if your bum bag is full) for a long drawn out 5-mile climb to the final ridge. Be careful here because the path is only a short breadth from a steep drop but then, once you've run past a delightful medieval gateau the route descends gently all the way to the finish but watch your step as you negotiate the rocks and boulders that litter the path. They could easily cause you to fall or twist an ankle, giving you a touch of the 'rock aches'. If you can set a marathon PB over this sort of course, you'll be the toast of your running club.

I am grateful to marathon runners Peter Bredd, his brother Ginger and their athletic grandmother, Nan, for the crumby review of this marathon and the 36 puns contained within, even though they were unable to sneak in the word crumpet.

Runner's riddle

Complete the sentence below with the right sportswear company, choosing one of the names from the list.

Athletes buy computer designed equipment from glamorous
....

Nike, Adidas, Hi-Tec, Asics, New Balance, Mizuno, Saucony, Brooks
(See page 192 for answer)

My first London Marathon

The training done, it wasn't always fun,
Early morning runs without the sun,
Rain, sleet, cold and snowing,
For six long months the biting wind blowing.

Then around it came, the big day had arrived,
The flu, the colds, the viruses – I'd survived,
I'm at the start line, huddled in the crowd,
Oh, if I can do this won't I feel proud?

We're off! the Wombles, the clown, the Viking ship,
The rhino, the trees, the banana – don't slip,
The crowds are so loud. The hoots and the cheers,
A couple of fairies stop off for some beers.

A group of policemen run after a crook,
A man in a bear suit, and then Captain Hook,
The miles pass by. I spot a friend,
Tower Bridge is around the bend.

Brilliant! Half way! We're on our way back,
To a hug, a kiss, a cuppa, a snack,
15, 16, 17 miles done,
18, 19, 20 I've run.

Oh no, it's the wall! I've heard about that,
But I'd followed Runner's World advice so forget about that,
21, 22, 23, the dreaded cobbles,
Look out! Smile at the camera and try not to wobble.

Smile! OK, grin! As you pass on your way,
Onto the finish and you hope and pray,
Along the Embankment, a couple get wed,
Oh God, I could do with my bed!

Big Ben strikes! No more breath to talk,
Around the bend into Bird Cage Walk,
The crowd going wild, the noise doesn't diminish,
Down the Mall onto the finish.

Arms in the air, tears rolling down,
Yes, I can do it, I can beat that clown,
Under the arch, over the line,
I've done it! 26 miles and I feel fine.

By Debbie Pentland

Ode to having lost something

Has anyone here seen my speed?
It was something that helped me to lead
A great many races,
At very fast paces,
Just like my good friend, Bob Eade.

Has anyone here seen my speed?
'Cos it's something I really do need,
I want to run fast,
Like I did in the past,
And not like a slow millipede.

After 30-odd years on the run,
Including some races I won,
I find that I'm slower,
And slower and slower,
Though I still find it ever such fun.

I know I should not be complaining,
That the lack of sufficient good training,

Is making me slow,
'Cos I know I should go
Out running even when it's raining.

I must never give in
To strained calf or bruised shin,
And make sure that I run with a smile,
For mile after mile after mile after mile,
Whatever the speed I am runnin'.

by Martin Bulger

And from another poet and playwright

"Things won are done; joy's soul lies in the doing." from
Shakespeare's Troilus & Cressida.

I don't know about you but I think this line suggests old Bill
Shakespeare was a marathon runner!

A cautionary tale

A few years ago, an old friend of mine and marathon fanatic, Phil Beacon, who I'd first met on the South Downs near Lewes in East Sussex, had an unfortunate accident. It happened when his neighbour, Mrs. Bowlegs went on holiday and he was asked to look after Spot, her pet zebra. While dismounting Spot, after having taken him for a ride over the Downs, he sprained his ankle quite badly. Anna, (that's Mrs. Bowlegs) was away for three weeks and Phil's ankle was giving him problems with his mobility, which was most annoying because he was due to take part in the local marathon on the coming Sunday. He was very concerned about his weak ankle and whether it could stand up to the rigours of the marathon, which was off-road.

Phil had strapped it up but that didn't seem to help much, and felt that he needed something much more rigid. He searched his house for some thin steel rods that he could lash to his weak ankle but couldn't find anything, and so decided to check Anna's house. He found nothing downstairs but as he was going upstairs, he spotted the metal bits that keep the stair carpet in place.

"Perfect," he said to himself, and he carefully removed them, with the intention of putting them back after the marathon with Anna none the wiser. Phil then strapped them to his injured ankle and tried them out with a quick jog round the block. The rods worked brilliantly, enabling him to run confidently and fast despite the injury, just what he knew he'd need for the rough terrain of the forthcoming marathon.

On race day he arrived suitably kitted out, and with the added assistance of the stair rods ran very well. In fact, Phil Beacon won the race but there was an objection regarding what was seen as an unfair advantage. The outcome of the complaint was that he was disqualified for taking Anna Bowlegs' stair rods.

Chapter 6

A Short Story

IN THE LONG RUN

It wasn't the most conventional way to take a holiday, not that backpacking could be considered unconventional, but it was the means of travel that made it rather unusual. You see, Jack was one of those odd types who found marathon running not only challenging but also fun to do, which is why after countless races over the 26.2 miles distance and a few even longer events, he decided on a running holiday.

Picking out places to visit, then running about thirty miles a day to see them, may have sounded the height of madness but in Jack's mind it was a great idea, so one evening after work he sifted through his pile of OS maps and devised a likely route that would take him about 200 miles in six days.

Jack's work colleagues all knew of his running exploits, either through having sponsored him to run a particular marathon, raising funds for a children's charity or frequently seeing him turn up for work in his jogging gear with his work clothes stuffed in the rucksack on his back.

Most of them had long since given up trying to understand Jack's love of running marathons but still managed to smile when one day he wore a T-shirt emblazoned with the bizarre slogan, *I've run loads of marathons and could tell you how, when and where but not why*. He was not a fitness freak but just someone who loved to run and who believed that the human body was designed to run, and run all day.

"It's easy," he said in the staffroom the next day, as he explained his running holiday plans for the following week. "It's just a question of breaking down the daily distances into manageable, bite-sized runs, and all done at a leisurely pace."

Jack paused to take a sip of his tea.

"Go on then," said Richard, sceptically, "explain your idea further, I'm intrigued."

"OK, I will," he replied, wearing one of his excited smiles. "Each day will probably begin with about a 10-mile run then I'll stop for a mid-morning snack, and do eight or so more miles before lunch. In the afternoon I'll walk a few miles then jog six more before taking another break. The last section will be comfortably slow and easy until I reach my destination."

"You make it all sound so easy," said a bewildered Doug, who was always quick to tease, "but I think you're mad, absolutely mad, and need locking up until you're prepared to be normal, like me and... like me. Don't you agree, Richard old chap?"

Richard stared at Jack for a few brief moments before smiling sympathetically at Doug.

"Perhaps he should consider politics as a career," he replied, "something like the Marathon Raving Loony Party would suit, I think."

"You realise that after a week of all that running, Jack, you'll need to come back to work for a rest," added Sue, with an air of resigned acceptance in her voice.

Meanwhile, Harry who had been half-following the conversation just looked up from his newspaper, glanced at Jack and slowly shook his head before returning to his crossword.

Undeterred by such words of encouragement, he spent the following weekend finalising the route then packing and repacking his rucksack to be ready for a Monday morning start.

It was late May and the countryside colours looked fresh and vibrant under the bright morning sun as Jack, bursting with anticipation, set out from his Salisbury home and headed along quiet roads towards Swanage. His efforts to keep the weight of the rucksack to a minimum yet adequately filled for six days of running had taken much deliberation but still left him with a heavy load on his shoulders, so at every opportunity he ran on the grass verge and occasionally followed footpaths and bridleways to escape the soulless hard-impact roads and pavements. This added extra miles to the journey but it didn't matter because as he told his friends at the Running Club, "It's not a race, no one's timing me so I can run at whatever pace I want, stop whenever I like and go wherever I please."

The skill of the long distance runner kicked in after a few miles when Jack's body seemed to ease into automatic and the rhythmic, almost musical, steady strides carried him effortlessly past tree-lined fields of corn and lush pastures of contented sheep and cattle. The sheer beauty of the countryside absorbed him as he cruised by the hedgerows, observing the rich changing tapestry of wild flowers, shrubs, busy insects and rustic fences, and partly-exposed rugged root systems of beech, hawthorn and holly. He was enjoying too, a sense of privilege that Nature's theatre was seeming to be performing just for him, and in no time at all he had reached the small village of Cranborne and made his first stop of the day.

He paused long enough to quench his thirst, munch his way through a snack bar and absorb some of the quiet beauty of the village, then he set off again – first just walking, then gradually easing into a gentle jog until he found his own instinctive and economical pace. Mile after mile he ran along lanes so quiet and empty that he was tempted to stray from the edge and run along the crown of the road and he would have done so but for a cyclist who cruised past him just as he was about to move into the middle.

"Morning," he called out, realising that he'd not spoken to anyone since the night before in the pub.

The cyclist, a young woman sporting khaki shorts, white T-shirt and a red and black striped cycle helmet raised her hand and turned her head just slightly to acknowledge his greeting and carried on.

This momentary communication with another human being seemed to go to his head as he pushed his pace up a gear, and for a few hundred metres he found himself trying to match her speed, but then the heavy rucksack and a slight rise in gradient forced him to see sense and drop back to his cruise speed not hers. Then suddenly, just before she disappeared from view he called out, but really only just above a whisper, "I love you, cyclist lady…"

Now this was unusual because Jack was not noted for reckless abandon and such spontaneity of emotion. All right, he liked to be adventurous and was always game for a laugh but yelling out like that, even quietly, was just not Jack. Then he glanced across at the enormous oak tree that he was just jogging past.

"Well, mighty oak, you saw her didn't you. I'm sure she was pretty and wasn't that a sun-tanned face and beaming smile I glimpsed? Tell her to wait for me... what's that you're rustling to me? 'Tis only the loneliness of the long distance runner talking. Perhaps you're right."

Jack felt a few moments of sadness and stared ahead wondering if she might return.

"Never mind," he sighed, as his thoughts then drifted slowly to the camaraderie he'd often experienced with people who share a love of sport. He'd lost count of the brief friendships forged while running a marathon, when invariably there'd come a point in the race where he'd be running at the same pace as someone else and would become engrossed in a conversation on all manner of things. That friendship could last a mile or for the rest of the race and would usually end with a handshake, respectful nod or occasionally a 'well-done hug'.

The approaching road sign told him that he'd reached the delightful town of Wimborne Minster, his planned stopping place for lunch. This was an opportunity for Jack to pamper himself just a bit and to re-fuel with a much-needed energy-packed meal, washed down with whatever beer the locals were drinking. He knew that in order to meet his target of about 30 miles a day, it was very important to keep his energy levels topped up because simple stamina and the determination to keep going 'when the going got tough' was not enough. Jack had already covered about 20 miles and was in no hurry to rush off after his meal so he sat by the river and casually read a newspaper until he felt fully recovered. He then checked the map, gave his legs a gentle massage then began the next part of his journey, the road to Poole.

He was quick to notice that the peace and quiet of the country lanes he'd run along during the morning had been replaced by the noises of a busy bustling road but his running still felt easy, although the strong sun made him wish for the sort of tree cover he'd enjoyed earlier in the day. However, the miles seemed to pass by quick enough and the thought of treating himself to a huge ice cream when he reached the seafront kept him focused. Jack loved everything about the sea and was feeling at peace with the world as he jogged along the road that skirted Poole harbour. The tangy smell of the sea air as it blew in across the sandy beach was tinged with the aroma of hot sand, sun tan oil and salty seaweed, and to his right clattered the rigging of a thousand moored dinghies, while dotted around the shallow waters were splashing children happily enjoying their half-term break. He bought a well-deserved ice cream on the seafront at Sandbanks and another as he walked the short distance to the ferry that would take him across the entrance to Poole Harbour.

He arrived at the ferry crossing point just as it was pulling away from the shore but he knew that it would be back again very soon so he sat down by the barrier to wait. He was just about to close his eyes against the glare of the sun when he caught a glimpse of one of the passengers on the ferry wearing a cycle helmet and white T-shirt. He jumped to his feet and strained his eyes but the ferry was moving away too fast. He could feel his pulse rate shoot up as he blurted out a futile, "Stop," then "Come back..." and then with a fading voice, "I thought I saw ... no, it couldn't be ... anyway, she'd be miles away by now."

He kept staring as the ferry crossed the narrow strait of water that linked Bournemouth Bay with Poole harbour. It was a busy thoroughfare for most of the day with fishing boats, huge cross-channel ferries, the small local ferry and pleasure craft of every shape and size, all creating a stunning panorama of marine activity. He sat down again, feeling slightly agitated but realising that his mind was probably just playing tricks. The ferry returned, the cars and foot passengers streamed off and Jack stepped aboard. Minutes later, the ferry had crossed over to the other side and he walked down the gangplank and on to terra firma once more. He was looking forward to completing his first day's running so immediately broke into a gentle jog. It was mid afternoon and the sun was as hot as ever as he padded his way along the soft white sand that covered the roadside path.

"Hey, gotta drink?"

Jack stopped within two strides and looked across the road at the young woman who'd just called out to him.

"I... I didn't recognise you without your cycle helmet," said a more than pleasantly surprised Jack. It was his cyclist lady.

"What?" she replied with a puzzled look.

"You passed me just south of Cranford," he added.

"Oh... yes...I remember now... the jogger with the rucksack. Have you run all the way here?"

Jack removed his rucksack and took out a couple of energy drinks.

"Here," he said with a smile, handing her one of them, "what's up – puncture?"

"Worse than that I'm afraid," she said despondently, "I've just had my bike stolen."

"Oh no," he said feeling genuinely taken aback, "how did...?"

"It all happened so quickly. I just leaned my bike up against this post then walked over there to watch the cross-channel ferry pass by. I looked back and it was gone, the bike, helmet and luggage, the lot, gone, like it had all just vanished into thin air. I looked up the road but there was no one on a bike pedalling away. I can only guess that a van must have pulled up alongside and waltzed off with it."

"That's rotten luck," he said sadly. "By the way, I'm Jack, marathon runner extraordinaire and occasional cyclist. Loves ice cream, Mozart... and oak trees. At the moment, running wherever my legs take me."

They shook hands.

"Oh... right... I'm Robbi, that's short for Roberta, on a cycling holiday but minus a bike. Occasional runner, possessing nothing but this bum bag and what I'm wearing now."

Jack looked at her closely. There appeared to be a dried tear stain down the side of her face or perhaps it was the perspiration from cycling in the hot weather. She had a lovely face but no beaming smile. Her hair was short and looked sun-bleached from all the cycling she'd probably done. He felt a strong urge to put a comforting arm around her, but didn't.

"Look," he said thoughtfully, "I was planning on having a quick swim off shell beach, just over there then jogging along the

South West Coast path to Swanage, I'm booked in at the Youth Hostel there and ..."

"You are?" she interrupted. "Me too."

Her missing smile began to return and Jack could feel himself going weak at the knees.

"Why... um... don't you join me, at least until Swanage. It'll give you time to gather your wits and time to plan what you're going to do tomorrow."

Robbi thought for a few moments then smiled again.

"OK then," she said, sounding remarkably cheerful after her devastating setback, "why not. So, where's this beach you mentioned, it sounds a lovely place."

Jack and Robbi ambled the short distance past bushes and sand dunes to the beach.

"You have a swim," said Robbi, still with a hint of sadness in her voice, "I'll just have a paddle here at the water's edge."

Jack smiled at her and then scanned the sparkling blue sea.

"Look at that," he said, pointing with a open hand, "have you ever seen such a beautiful sight. Come on, we can both have a swim, I can lend you a towel and some dry clothes for afterwards. I'm sure you're dying to cool off properly after your cycling."

For several minutes Robbi continued to stare at the dazzling sea then she looked back at Jack again and nodded.

"You're right, it is beautiful," she replied, "and I could certainly do with a swim right now, OK."

"You know, there's a lot to be said for taking a refreshing dip in the briny to clear one's head," said Robbi, as she surfaced next to Jack about thirty metres off shore.

"Yeah, you're right," he responded, in his soft calming voice, "and can there be a lovelier spot in Britain to do it?"

"So Jack, how far is it to Swanage then, I'll need to buy a few things there?" asked Robbi.

"Oh, only about seven miles...ish by road," he replied, "but infinitely more enjoyable would be the coastal path. Mind you, if we walk it, the shops may be shut by the time we get there, so do you feel up to a gentle jogging pace?"

"Seven miles you say…? mm… well. I suppose as long as you don't go too fast then," she smiled.

"No chance," he said, "I've already done 27 miles today so I promise it will be nothing more than what I call 'easy pace, admire the views'."

They waded ashore and spent a short while sunbathing before getting kitted out and setting off. They ran close to the water's edge to begin with where the sand was firm because further up the beach the glorious sand, speckled with a million shells, though great for sunbathing and hurling the odd Frisbee, was too soft to run on.

They were both unusually quiet for the first few miles, perhaps captivated by the beauty around them and probably musing about other things too. Actually, Robbi was deep in thought over the incident that had brought to an abrupt end her mid-term escape from the primary school classes that she taught. One moment she was on top of the world, enjoying a delightful day's cycling through picturesque countryside in weather that was a foretaste of a hot summer, then suddenly, the whole holiday was washed away like a child's sandcastle disappearing under an incoming wave.

"What should I do," she wondered, "catch a bus back home tomorrow morning, defeated by an opportunist thief or perhaps stay on in Swanage for the rest of the week… and then catch a bus home?" She sighed.

"You OK?" asked Jack.

"Yeah, fine, just thinking, that's all," she replied with a smile.

Jack had been thinking too, replaying the events of the day over and over in his head, in particular, that chance meeting, that one in a million chance meeting, well, not even a meeting, just a few seconds of time on an empty lane somewhere in Dorset. Then a fleeting glimpse of her again, and then the bike theft. If he believed in destiny, he would have to say that fate had stepped in and he was meant to meet her.

He glanced across at Robbi as she matched him stride for stride and smiled at the sight of her in his running shorts and T-shirt. He looked again. She may have described herself as an 'occasional runner' but to Jack she seemed to be a natural. Her relaxed comfortable style looked in perfect harmony with her body as she ran with all the grace and confidence of a true athlete.

'Would this be,' he thought, 'just another of his *marathon friendships*, one that would end in Swanage with a handshake or hug? Please let it be a hug. I suppose only time will tell.'

They left the beach and followed a track that took them up and round the headland, where the eastern end of the Purbeck Hills meets the sea in spectacular fashion by the Old Harry Rocks.

Shortly afterwards, they both jogged onto the seafront at Swanage and slowed to a walk.

"Well done, Robbi," smiled Jack, "you're a natural runner."

"Thanks Jack, thanks for lifting me out of my gloom back there and thanks too for showing me the thrill of running. It's... it's like being a completely free spirit, like you're in total control of your body and your life. Now I know why I see so many runners wearing a smile when they finish a race or fun run. It's not just about completing the distance, is it? It's more because a sort of incredible feel-good factor that's almost bursting out of you."

Jack nodded, "I know what you mean."

They walked further along the seafront then wandered through the town, and a few shops later, Robbi had bought a small rucksack and replaced some of the things that had disappeared with her bike, then the two of them headed up the road towards the hostel.

"Listen," said Robbi quietly, "I've been thinking."

Oh no... thought Jack, what will it be, the handshake or the hug? "No, wait a minute," he interrupted, firmly, "I've been thinking too, and... I'd like to take you out for a meal this evening. Do you accept the invitation?"

"That's just what I was going to say," said Robbi, "but yes, thank you. I accept."

It was right at the end of the meal when they were on their final coffee that Robbi put her cup down and whispered,

"So, where shall we run to tomorrow?"

Chapter 7

Running Holidays & Ultra Marathons

The short story (previous chapter) is based on a running holiday that I had many years ago, although in reality it did not involve the lady cyclist and in referring to it as a running holiday it should not be confused with 'running holidays' organised by some tour companies.

The idea of having a running holiday first emerged while my family and I were staying in Stoneleigh, near Coventry for a week's holiday. Exploring quiet country lanes and footpaths that took in Kenilworth, Warwick, the Grand Union Canal and a host of small villages was a most pleasant change from my usual routes around the South Downs and the Sussex Coast. So enjoyable was the experience that it made me want to explore even more areas on the OS map that I had brought with me. Could I run to Rugby and Daventry then back to Stoneleigh or perhaps Stratford-upon-Avon and down to Banbury? The mind was racing and the finger tracing a likely route on the map moved easily and with great, though unrealistic, adventure. That evening when I scanned the pages of the road atlas in my car, I realised that Oxford didn't look too far... and of course, Oxford is near to Reading... and Reading... well... is close to Guildford... then Crawley... and that's almost back home! I can't remember anything about my run the following day because my mind had been captivated by the notion of running home from Stoneleigh to Seaford. All I had to do was break it to my wife, Shirley and my children that, at the end of our holiday, while they were driving back to Seaford, I would be running home, a distance of 170 miles.

With a rucksack economically packed for five days of running my aim was to use as many minor roads as possible and to take it all at a leisurely pace. As the short story recounted, I would divide the day up into four sessions, none more than 90 minutes in length.

My daily destinations were Stow-on-the-Wold (35 miles), the Ridgeway just south of Wantage (30 miles), Bracknell (35 miles), South Nutfield, near Redhill (35 miles) and finally Seaford (42 miles) staying at youth hostels or B&Bs on the way.

Marathon running can open the door to a lifetime of enjoyment and good health but there can also be unexpected spin-offs. Running holidays for instance, can put your marathon running skills to another use. Consider this. Zero travel costs, no traffic queues and seeing the countryside close up. Raising the next town... and the next under your own steam heightens the experience of travelling and increases the sense of achievement. I found the navigating at a slow running speed quite easy, and fun, although the desire to avoid main roads wherever possible created quite a meandering route and therefore added extra miles. Because it wasn't a marathon race of 26.2 miles with a known 'set of rules' of how to run it, the mindset that I had to tune into for a running holiday was rather different. Without restrictions, other than the need to reach my destination before nighttime, it became more of an adventure, with more chance to enjoy the countryside and the simple pleasures in life. I always began each day very slowly, which helped the legs to ease into the gentle, rhythmic pace that enabled me to complete that section of the journey fairly comfortably. Each of the two snack breaks were relaxed, generous affairs, unlike the snatched glass of water, piece of orange or biscuit in a marathon race, and the lunch time stop became an hour or so of sheer indulgence, a pub meal (including pudding) and wine or beer. Definitely not the done thing in a normal marathon but certainly acceptable on a running holiday.

After lunch and a spot of TLC leg massaging and stretching I'd walk for 30 minutes then begin again, totally refreshed. It was so easy, with any tiredness being brushed aside by the fun of exploring new places.

Despite the distance covered in those five days, there just wasn't the tiredness normally associated with the after effects of even one marathon. This encouraged me to do it again the following year, but over a completely different route.

It was also different in that it involved my eldest son, Graham, who was 13 at the time. While I ran, he cycled, with our two rucksacks fixed to the back of his bike. Our route was also more adventurous as it included running abroad. We went along the south coast from Seaford through Eastbourne, Hastings and Rye to Folkestone (two days of running) then took the ferry across to Boulogne. From there it was another two days of running to reach Dieppe before another ferry brought us to Newhaven, leaving just a short hop from there to Seaford. Our abiding memory of that running holiday was the two days in France, in particular, the inconsistent information on the road signposts. Too often for it to be coincidental we would note the distance as being, for instance, 10 km to the next town then 20 minutes later see a sign that said it was 11 km to go. This can be very demoralising when you're tired and hungry...! And I can assure you that we hadn't taken a wrong turning.

In 1995 it was my other son, David's turn. He was just 13, and again we followed a different route, taking the Newhaven ferry to Dieppe but then going west towards Cherbourg. Adventurously, our target on the first day was Honfleur, a distance of about 65 miles and it included going over the River Seine on the newly-opened Pont de Normandie, a spectacular and stunning piece of engineering, the most amazing bridge I've ever run over! Unfortunately, the French road sign saga emerged again to thwart our Herculean efforts. Perhaps the bridge was so new that they hadn't properly sorted out the signposting because when we reached it, it appeared to offer no pedestrian access, even though I'd bravely telephoned the Le Havre Tourist Information Office before setting off, to check that the bridge was open to walkers/runners and cyclists. I remembered from a previous spot of cycling in France that the Pont de Tancarville was the nearest alternative so David and I had no option but to head for that bridge. Two hours later we reached a town and because it was almost dark by then we decided to book into a hotel and rethink our plans. The following morning with assurances from the hotel manager that the Pont de Normandie was crossable, we retraced our steps and after much searching found a small road through an industrial estate that took us to the bridge. We eventually reached Cherbourg and crossed the channel to Poole, having covered a mere 200 miles in four days. This was more than just a holiday because it was specifically timed for me to do the **Poole Marathon** the following day. In what seemed like a sauntering pace I clocked 3:33 while David, who was also a useful runner, entered the mini run attached to the main event and picked up a trophy for second place. The following day David caught the train home while I cycled his bike back to Seaford (a distance of 110 miles).

This glut of physical activity had another motive as it formed the crucial 'peak' in my preparation for the South Downs Way 80 miles race. It was no coincidence that my time for that ultra, 12 hours 42 minutes, was not only my PB for the race by more than two hours but it was also achieved so easily that I could have run it again the next day. If I had to single out just one race in which I felt I had achieved my perfect wave, this was it, and interestingly, I ran the last 79 miles on my own. For anyone who runs marathons I would recommend this sort of holiday, either for the five-star enjoyment and freedom factor or as an easy way into ultras… or both.

The opportunity for my daughter, Claire, to do something similar when she was thirteen came and went, unfulfilled. However, the chance for her to share my love of distance running will be satisfied when she runs her first marathon, at the **Beachy Head** event. The timing of her first one (close to her twenty-first birthday) will enrich both events, and is perhaps reminiscent of my hundredth marathon which I did on my fiftieth birthday… but this is not a quirk of the Bulger household.

Jenny Cobby of Henfield Joggers ran her first marathon close to her fiftieth birthday. Bill Young of the Seaford Striders celebrated his seventieth birthday by completing his hundredth marathon (at London 2006)… and there are many, many more examples round the country of runners who have enjoyed similar number junctions (or memorable milestones). I wonder why that is! Could it be that, like it or not, our '26 miles 385 yards' sport is jam packed and inextricably involved with numbers. We think about our speed in miles per hour, and our split times, lap times and our mile pace feature in our thoughts as we seek to measure our progress. We might run three or four times a week, go out for 30, 50 or 90 minutes, clocking up 20, 40 or 60 miles each week, and if our marathon finishing time is 2:59:59 instead of 3:00:00, that single second difference is the same emotionally, psychologically and actually as receiving a FA Cup winner's medal rather than a runners-up piece of metal.

The Grand Union Canal – 145 miles

The fickle finger of fate can sometimes get so firmly stuck in the ear of some runners that it seems to dislodge the part of the brain associated with sanity and the ability to say "stop, that's enough." Well, whatever it is that drives a runner to run more than a marathon, there are plenty of events to satisfy that madness.

When I'd done seventy-seven marathons, the South Downs Way 80 miles four times and the classic 'London to Brighton' once, I noticed in my RRC race directory an even greater challenge, the Grand Union Canal race from Birmingham to London. My first thought was that it would be flat or gently downhill all the way. After all, whoever heard of a river going uphill? I curse my ignorance. How was I to know that the organiser would conjure up a hill? (It happened when the canal went into a very long tunnel and the runners had to go up and over) and canal locks can take a 'river' uphill.

Unfortunately, for the last few years, through demands at work and injuries, my training had been meagre for too long so if I was going to take up this challenge I would have to increase my training, do more cycling and swimming and most importantly, lose some weight.

I sent off my entry form and cheque to help focus my attention on some suitable preparation. I told my club and instantly received an offer to be my support crew. Others questioned my sanity and suitability to remain as club captain.

Like most of my recent racing, I'd treat it as a training run but at what pace and what was the deterioration rate over a distance of 145 miles? In my mind it was simply a matter of running five and a half marathons in a row. With expert maths and total ignorance I imagined I'd do 6mph for 10 hours, 5mph for the next 10 hours and 4mph for the last part. Add an hour or so for major food stops and I'd do it in about 31 hours. However, such brash logic would also make me the first runner to break 2 hours for the **London Marathon**. My general training didn't improve, though I did try. I blame an Achilles problem that wouldn't go away and a funny knee that wasn't funny at all, not forgetting a five-star stress situation at work.

Ill-prepared was the fool who did four marathons in quick succession as preparation then lined up at the start in Gas Street Basin, Birmingham with twelve other runners at 6am Saturday 24th May for the 1997 Grand Union Canal Run. I didn't know what the others were thinking but I was thinking that I'd not really had any sleep although I had planned everything precisely... which didn't explain why I'd left the maps of the route at home. Fortunately, I was able to purchase replacement maps and receive a few words of encouragement from race organiser, Dick Kearn.

"Off you go then," said the starter, quietly.

The cool, calm and sunny conditions seemed perfect as we set off in silence along the towpath. Birmingham seemed so peaceful and green, and just to prove it, I saw my first ever kingfisher. For someone who had lived all his life in rural parts of Hampshire and Sussex it came as a total surprise to see one while still within the city limits of Birmingham.

For a while I ran with Joan Clarke, the only lady competitor and then Gary from Bristol but after 10 miles I was on my own and glad to meet up at various points with Mel Allen, a fellow Seaford Strider who had driven me up to Birmingham and who also had had very little sleep. He kept me topped up with bananas, drink and much needed encouragement.

I remember stopping after 20 miles and sitting down on the edge of the canal for 5 minutes, uncertain of just what I had got myself into. My head was buzzing with confusion and doubt, but then reality seemed to kick in. I was miles from home, I had 125 miles still to run and giving up was not an option so I stood up and carried on. The tow path of a canal can be a delightful place to run, with stunning pastel-shaded scenery contrasting vividly with the bright, colourful narrow boats which chugged majestically along at a serene 4mph. I'd frequently see one in the distance and slowly pull it in, then overtake it like it was a slower runner. This proved to be psychologically quite beneficial as the rest of the runners were nowhere to be seen. Keeping focused for such an unbelievably long time was vital and was helped by Mel popping up every 5 or 10 miles with snacks, drink and badly-needed moral support. The first real low was shortly after 26 miles when I could sense my legs saying, "OK, I've got you round a marathon. Can we stop now?" That strange sensation has happened to me in all seven of my ultras. As someone once said, "your legs have a memory." You train your legs to run marathons and they develop a memory of the distance, regardless of the time taken, so when you venture beyond 26 miles, they know... and complain. It may then take a few miles for your legs to accept what's going on but eventually they understand and provided you keep them fed and watered they'll carry you to the finish.

At 50 miles I caught up with Ron Pattenden, who was struggling with an injury so I stayed with him, jogging and walking to the 70 mile-checkpoint. It was here that Ron 'gave up' and I sat in a car for about 40 minutes. It was dark and Mel decided to have a kip in his car as my second support crew, my wife, Shirley, Claire, my daughter and Eric, my father-in-law, had arrived to take over. Although I had rigged up a sort of miners' lamp for the next leg of the race, I didn't need it as there was a full moon and clear sky. Eric joined me as a 'buddie' as we walked through the night until shortly after daybreak when he 'stood down' and I carried on alone. It was then that I began to have real problems, not with my legs but because it was Sunday morning and I hadn't slept since Thursday night. The sun, which had blazed down on me unremittingly for the whole of Saturday was doing the same again, and I couldn't keep my eyes open. Yet, if I closed them for a second I was certain to stumble into the waiting canal. We have probably all done a marathon in hot weather, suffering up to 6 hours of strong sun, so imagine the effect of 15 hours on two consecutive days. Somehow I managed to make it to the 100-mile point and there, had a total MOT and overhaul – massage, fresh kit, food, drink and a wash. Mel took over as support crew again and I started running again. I stopped at 119 miles for another massage, food and drink and, with only a marathon to go began to sense success. Ron, who'd 'given up' earlier rejoined me but as a support runner, a 'buddy', and it was his patience and quiet encouragement that, on reflection, was so vital when later, I descended into my lowest 'low'. Short spells of running became even shorter until finally at about 134 miles I stopped. The sun was still fierce and unforgiving, and I hated it. I felt that not only was my fuel tank empty but my reserve tank (my inner strength) was too. All dials on my physical and mental dashboard were reading zero. I yearned to sleep and for perhaps half an hour lay by the side of the canal. Although I was on the point of losing it completely, my subconscious must have been alert and searching the brain furiously for a way to override the state I was in...

Then for no apparent reason I stood up and began to walk... then jog and walk... which then became a continuous slow jog. At about 138 miles I stopped for a quick snack and to put on some extra clothes. I resumed my jogging which then imperceptibly increased in pace. I remember Ron saying that if we kept it up, we might even dip under the 40 hour mark. The all-encompassing 'low' that I had been stuck in seemed to have been forgotten and I was not tired anymore. Maybe my subconscious had refused to accept another night on my feet and no sleep because I was not jogging, but running and I maintained a good speed until the last 500 metres when I found another gear and sprinted into Little Venice and the finishing line. Bizarrely after that ultimate 'low' I had managed to reinvent myself and run the last 7 miles in 55 minutes to give me a finishing time of 39 hours and 55 minutes. I then discovered that my finishing position was fourth, and last, the other runners having, for various reasons, pulled out.

Although my training for this amazing challenge was woefully inadequate, what counted in the end was the selfless dedication of my two support crews, Eric's companionship through Saturday night and Sunday morning, Ron's crucial support over the last 30 miles and a stubborn streak in me that knew no limits. I'm glad I did it and am fairly certain that I will never do it again but if I'm mad enough to do it once...

Martin Bulger

The South Downs Way – 80 miles

When the Felbridge Junior Rugby team, from near Tunbridge Wells, needed new equipment for their club, Harry Townsend decided to organise a long distance race to raise funds. Starting just south of Petersfield in Hampshire the route would follow the South Downs Way for 80 miles, finishing at Eastbourne in East Sussex. Little did he realise just how popular this event would become and how, even though it no longer exists, it's still talked about with such affection and enthusiasm.

Each year it would start at 9 a.m. on the Saturday nearest to the longest day, ensuring the maximum possible hours of daylight running. It is accepted that it did not have the ruggedness of say, the West Highland Way in Scotland, yet it was still an extremely demanding course. Some runners used to describe it as three Seven Sisters Marathons in a row, which is a pretty accurate way of looking at it.

In a field opposite the Queen Elizabeth Country Park, 10 miles north of Portsmouth, there would be tents, camper vans and caravans belonging to runners who had arrived the day before. Closer to the road is the car park that would begin to fill up from 6 a.m. and three hours later would be the starting line for 400 runners, joggers and fast walkers, all aiming to complete the course inside the 25-hour limit.

The race itself began by following the underpass to the other side of the busy A3, to join a track that climbed steadily through the forest. The vexatious background hum of the traffic quickly disappeared to be replaced by peaceful birdsong and quiet but excited chatter. I can only ever remember warm sunny race days though there must have been a few damp ones but what is not in any doubt is the memory of the picturesque and ever-changing scenery that was a constant companion and inspiration. Running through the quiet, restful calm of the South Downs countryside on a sunny, Saturday morning empowered you with a belief that you could run for ever, which was quite fortunate because some runners would still be running 24 hours later. Soft, comfortable running along woodland paths and over huge grassy tracts of severely undulating downland and through the occasional farm and village community should have been fairly easy on the eye and limb but the frequently flint-strewn, rutted chalk trails made it necessary for runners to concentrate continually to avoid turned ankles, a task that was made tougher than normal because of the strong reflected glare off the white expanses of uncovered chalk, exacerbated by the strong day-long sun.

The checkpoints along the route, anything between 3 and 9 miles apart, not only refreshed the body with food and drink but also, meeting up with your support crew at regular intervals was of immense psychological benefit – it would lift your flagging spirit and recharge your mental batteries. These selfless helpers, as in all other ultra races, are crucial to a runner succeeding, surviving unscathed and sustaining the will to carry on when every part of the runner is saying "Stop! I've had enough." They will often also assist lone runners too, offering them a similar degree of moral support, which can be a real life-saver. The early stages of the South Downs Way event tended to pass quite quickly, perhaps because runners were so engrossed in the enormity of the task ahead and the less well-known sensations of taking the body beyond 26.2 miles rather than thinking about the early part of the race… and anyway, the runner's reliable automatic pilot would have kicked in so all there was to do was to 'sit back' and enjoy the day. Checkpoints near to South Harting and Hill Top Farm consequently came and went, and it was only after Littleton Farm, when the route followed a 150-foot sharp climb back up on to the ridge, that runners were forced to think carefully about their speed and the degree of energy that they were prepared to expend at such an early stage of the race. Finding the right pace and sticking to it was a wise strategy for coping with the relentless climbs ahead.

The descent into the Arun River Valley is fairly steep and offers a clear view ahead of the town of Amberley with its busy road and rail routes squeezing through the gap in the Downs. Also visible is the route that the South Downs Way takes after the town but for some reason runners tended to concentrate instead on picking out the checkpoint. They would have covered 26 miles on reaching it but the usual elation at having run that distance was often muted compared with the feelings after completing an ordinary marathon. The long arduous climb out of Amberley that they had probably noticed from the other side of the valley ought to be called Rodin's Hill because I'm sure that many runners did a lot of thinking while they were forcing their bodies beyond the marathon distance and up on to the South Downs ridge once more. It is certainly steep enough to make most runners walk part of it but in doing so it would send messages to the brain that created a bizarre misunderstanding. The brain would receive two bits of information – that the legs had run 26 miles and that now it was walking – which it initially translated as having run a marathon and must therefore be walking back to the car or to the changing rooms for a shower. As a result, it would switch on to its 'close down' mode... but minutes later... lo and behold when the route levelled out a bit... the legs began to say "off we go again." The brain seemed to reply, "oh no we're not, we've finished... haven't we?" So the next section of the route, all the way to the restful checkpoint at Washington, which was at 32 miles, was for many therefore, a strange one as the body tried to persuade the brain that things were not what it thought this time. Eventually it would realise that something different was happening and resumed its involvement so that by the time the route passed Chanctonbury Ring the mind and body were back in harmony and running/jogging as if the previous 35 miles hadn't happened. The course then dropped steeply into the Adur Valley offering a similar vista to the one approaching Amberley but it was only when runners reached the river crossing that they would notice the mean-looking climb to the top of Truleigh Hill. They may or may not have been pleased to realise that they had just passed half-way and from then on they would have less to do than they'd done.

The major checkpoint at the top of Truleigh Hill offered a significant food and drink stop and perhaps a longer rest than usual... but not for too long, as the challenge ahead beckoned strongly. It was strange that despite the distance already done, runners seemed able to reinvent themselves for the second half of the race and eat up the miles once more with amazing ease. Perhaps it's a case of ultra runners developing the ability to switch on to automatic more easily and for longer periods.

You would pass the Devil's Dyke and the bridge and checkpoint at Pyecombe, run close to Jack and Jill, the Clayton Windmills and then conquer Ditchling Beacon, but before you crossed the A27 to the Newmarket Inn checkpoint between Brighton and Lewes, you would probably have worked out that there was barely a marathon to go. The spring in your stride was likely to return because of that realisation but would be quickly cancelled out when you had to negotiate yet another of the countless 200-foot ascents, this time taking you back up to the top of the Downs overlooking the village of Kingston. Some runners might have reached this point by nightfall while others would have passed by before teatime. The miles continued to be pulled in surprisingly easily perhaps because the brain was numb and the legs were still on autopilot... or vice versa!.. or both. At the Southease checkpoint by the foot of Itford Hill many runners would have decided to eat breakfast, whatever time it was that they reached it. Cornflakes never tasted so scrumptious as when you'd been running for 67 miles!

On my best SDW 80 my pace seemed to quicken once I reached Firle Beacon, probably because I was on home territory and knew every protruding tree root and rabbit hole; every blade of grass and most of the sheep by name... joke! From here, my support crew – my ever patient wife, Shirley – drove from checkpoint to checkpoint but could not keep up as I must have sensed the perfect wave and increased my pace yet further regardless of the steep bone-shaking drop into Alfriston, the long climb up to Windover Hill, the rugged hazardous descent into Jevington (usually done in the dark) and the last of the tough endless hills up to Butt's Brow. On the ridge high above Eastbourne, the runners' confidence would be sky-high and once you had survived the very tricky, flint-laden, stinging-nettled steep, winding drop to tarmac roads and civilisation the last kilometre would be covered on cloud nine and the finishing line greeted with the most overwhelming accumulation of emotions – an enormous sense of achievement mixed with a feeling of immense relief, bursting elation and even a twinge of sadness that the epic challenge was finally over.

Martin Bulger

******

Otter High Peak 40

In September 1992 several of my club colleagues and I were attracted to the Otter High Peak 40, a trail race in the Derbyshire Peak District. It was a long journey for us so we had to travel on the Friday evening but a well-chosen B&B in Buxton, only a few yards from the start and finish, got the weekend off to a good start, even though the landlord was not too impressed with our requirements for a very early breakfast, indeed I seem to recall we had to prepare most of it ourselves.

Early on the Saturday morning the Race HQ was seething with activity as some 270 or so runners registered and generally pottered about in that well known mixture of excitement and trepidation. We set off from the main street before the rush of Saturday morning shopping and soon disappeared into the hills, all clutching our very precious route descriptions. The morning was cool, rather grey, misty and slightly drizzly in Buxton, not bad at all for distance running, but it proved to be considerably worse elsewhere.

The queues at the first couple of stiles soon dissipated as the field spread out and it was not long before those of us with any ambitions of finishing towards the front were running alone. I hardly saw another runner for 30 miles. Although the major turns were marked, thankfully, the route description notes were essential for keeping on the correct paths in between times and locating the regular drinks stations around the course. The early miles were reasonably straightforward; hills not too steep, dry stone walls not too high, not too much mud and good visibility, in spite of the persistent drizzle. But then the trail began to climb Rushup Edge (very inaptly named because there was definitely no 'rushing up' this climb) towards Mam Tor and suddenly we were out of the drizzle and into thick fog with visibility down to less than 15 yards in places. We could all so easily have got completely lost along this stretch of open moorland had the organisers not had the foresight to listen seriously to the weather forecast and set out a series of flashing lights at regular intervals to direct us to Hollins Cross and the descent into Castleton. Sadly there was not a glimpse of the magnificent views northwards across the Edale Valley towards Kinder Scout, which is the southern end of the Pennine Way.

The big descent was pretty hair-raising too, particularly the first stretch in the fog. It was steep and rocky with sections of loose scree stones and several rushing streams to cross. This took us down below the heavy fog that mercifully did not return but there was still a thick mist on the higher stretches and an intermittent drenching drizzle elsewhere.

Through the edge of Castleton, I recall rather stupidly misreading the directions and losing a few precious minutes backtracking to find the entrance to Cave Dale. All the way the tracks were rocky and treacherous, just the sort of terrain that leads to turned ankles, or worse.

However, a bit of respite for the ankles came along the stretch of quiet road to Tideswell but then back off road again into the lovely conjoining valleys of Millers Dale, Upperdale and Monsal Dale with their disused remains of the water-driven Litton and Cressbrook Mills, derelict reminders of the industrial revolution. Across the A6 and into the first of two valleys known as Deep Dale. This Deep Dale number one was straight forward enough, with just one of those long climbs that seem to get steeper the further you go. Five miles further however, came Deep Dale number two, a much more difficult and memorable proposition. A fiendishly steep descent reduced most of us, certainly including me, to going down on our bottoms, while the equally fiendish climb up the other side required hands as well as legs to reach the top. If you don't believe me, just look at the OS map – the contour lines could hardly be any closer.

By this time the rather gloomy weather that had been threatening something really nasty ever since we came down from the fog had decided thankfully that the relentless drizzle was all it was going to do, but the later runners certainly had a pretty cold as well as damp finish to the day. The light was already beginning to deteriorate as I crossed the final grassy field and climbed the stile onto the road for the last mile or so into a grey and quiet Buxton and back to the HQ for a very welcome warm shower and a hot meal.

In their post-race report the organisers said how worried they were about competitors getting lost in the fog but thankfully, their foresight with lamps and a bit of fortunate (skilful) map reading by the runners meant everyone returned safely. Altogether a great day's sport and I had to be well satisfied with a finishing time of 6:33. My personal duel with club mate Graham was very close all the way. He stayed 2 or 3 minutes ahead all the way to 34 miles at which point I caught him. Sadly for me this spurred him into a surge of energy (he did not want to be beaten by an old man) and he pulled away to finish 4 minutes in front. Our small team all completed, with times ranging from 6:29 to 9:55 and when we finally regrouped for some serious fluid replacement it has to be admitted that it was not Buxton Spa Water that we were drinking.

John Gill

******

The Fat Ass 54 Fight The Flab Run Finishing In Farnham.

For some unknown reason I think the race organiser liked using as many F words as possible... either that or perhaps he was an alliteration junkie!

I don't really know quite why I was attracted to this event. Run on the first Sunday of the new year it was advertised as having "no support, no medals and no wimps". This was right, the only real support was a burger van and a can of beer at the finish, there were certainly no medals in sight and I tend to think that anyone tackling something like this has to have moved out of the land of wimps and into some sort of cloud-cuckoo land.

The approximate 54-mile run was run along the North Downs Way from Dunton Green Station, near Sevenoaks in Kent to Farnham Station in Surrey. Unfortunately the race rules did not permit the use of the train service, although it could well be that on that line in the middle of winter it may have been quicker to run.

Being quite close to the shortest day of the winter it was no surprise that an early start was the order of the day and fortunately at least one of my volunteer support duo – Dave the Driver and Ian the Map, had invested in an alarm clock and they arrived at my door at about 5:30 a.m. My pleas of injury, illness and lunacy fell on deaf ears and I was unceremoniously bundled into the car. Actually, they were rather inclined to believe my pleas of lunacy but thought it was too late for me to escape. I must have grabbed a little doze along the way because it was a major shock to the system when I was pushed out of the car at Dunton into the cold and dark an hour or more before any truly sensible mortal had even thought of leaving the comfort of a warm bed. I seriously wondered whether this was what friends were for. It really was very dark and very cold, measured, I was told at -6°C and falling, so full thermals were required. A motley crew we looked; 35 or so starters dressed in a strange and totally bizarre assortment of, we hoped, cold-beating clothing. Have you ever noticed what peculiar things runners wear in these circumstances?

The start was, to say the least, informal. The organisers, members of the Brighton Hash, enquired at about 7 a.m. if we were all ready. The immediate and unanimous reply of "No" was totally ignored and so to the rather off-hand command of "OK, let's go then," the watch was started and we were off. A race such as this cannot be marked all the way so the precious and, I must say, particularly excellent route description notes were of great importance, although they were hard to see for the first few miles. I could see the eventual winner, Stephen Moore, for the better part of 30 seconds before he disappeared into the darkness never to be seen by any of the competitors again as he finished an hour ahead of the next runners – the redoubtable Hillary Walker and clubmate Graham Lyall. The first glimmer of dawn came after about three quarters of an hour and not long after this I began to realise just how cold it was. There had not been any actual snow but everywhere was absolutely white: grass, hedges, trees, roads and even the clouds (ominously).

The run was mainly along the North Downs Way Long Distance Path, doubling at times as the Pilgrim's Way. This chalk Downs path is very different from the South Downs Way. The latter is almost entirely a ridgeway path with fine views to both north and south, while the North Downs version runs mainly along the foot or lower sections of the scarp. Mud was not a problem as everything was frozen solid and I was probably not too far from that state myself. However, it is surprising how a good steady plod does maintain the body's core temperature and it gradually became apparent that my support crew were colder than me and were reluctant to leave the car for long as they fed and watered me at regular intervals. This actually suited me as I have always believed that in an ultra event the last thing you should do is stop for longer than is absolutely necessary at the drinks points and certainly never sit down.

By mid morning the temperature had not changed noticeably, it may have just about reached zero, but the day had opened up into something really rather beautiful. For two or three hours the sky was an almost cloudless pale watery blue and the low sun lit up the ice and frost like a sort of fairyland. Frozen dew on spiders' webs and the myriads of dripping icicles on the trees and bushes seemed like a huge advertisement for crystal glassware. Meanwhile, the rhythmic crunch of the frosted grass underfoot testified that the miles were steadily passing.

The route description had kept me on track without any problems, indeed the first tricky patch was not experienced until the steep descent from the popular viewpoint of Box Hill, probably the highest point of the course, which was a bit slippery as the top layer of frost had at last melted away slightly. Thankfully we did not have to use the stepping stones at the bottom as they would have been a tricky and daunting hazard with tired legs and the River Mole looking very cold and unwelcoming. From here the route passed through some pleasant backways up to Ranmore Common and on to Newlands Corner, a favourite viewpoint just outside Guildford. We then passed onto St Martha's Hill, which is the starting point for another long distance footpath, The Downs Link, that goes south to the back of Shoreham-by-Sea.

At this point in the race, the chalk of the North Downs was left behind and a remarkably sandy stretch of countryside led onto a relatively flat finishing section to Farnham and a welcome rest. The last mile or two were completed with the light fading and the temperature returning to well below freezing. We finished as we had started, in the cold and dark. Cold fingers were not able to cope with shoe laces and other kit so I was helped out of my sweaty gear (yes, even in the cold it was sweaty running) and installed in the comfort of a warm car to taxi me home for a bath and a hot meal. The 'Fat Ass 54' was organised for several years in a rather low-key way but seems to have dropped out of the calendar now. A shame really because it was a memorable race in memorable conditions and I am sure many other ultra runners would have enjoyed the experience.

John Gill

Chapter 8

Contributors' Own Stories

Eric Hardwicke – Hastings Runners

Like most marathon runners, I became excited about the challenge with the advent of the first **London Marathon** in 1981. Before then it was seen as an extreme event which took place at the Olympic Games every four years, with heroes like Jim Peters and Emil Zatopek. Normal people just did not run marathons, but suddenly we were able to aspire to running this great distance, initially through the **London Marathon** then later, many more marathons.

Because I didn't gain an entry for the first **London Marathon** I decided to look elsewhere and chose the **Isle of Thanet Marathon** as my first one. I had only started running to improve my fitness for squash, then I came second in the squash club's New Year's Day Run and things seemed to snowball from there. As for the rest of my marathon training, I was very much on my own, doing my 'own thing' and I just made it up as I went along.

I fully believed that I was well-prepared for the **Isle of Thanet** and found the first half of the race along the seafront towards Reculver Castle and back over Manston Airport enjoyable and easy, reaching halfway in 2 hours. Then it hit me! Ramsgate, Broadstairs and the North Foreland became a hell that I had not experienced before. I had to drag my body up the steep hills out of these towns and places, with every part of me suffering. To take my mind off the pain, I sang my favourite songs as loud as I could and smiled. I will never forget the reaction of a family who were supporting another runner, who kept appearing at different points around the course. They applauded and encouraged me. When I neared the end of the marathon (and the end of my suffering) I asked them why they were giving me such fantastic support at every opportunity even though they didn't know me. With a mile to go they said that I looked so happy and they enjoyed my singing too. I clocked 5:45 and was so grateful to this family for getting me through my first marathon. Fortunately, my friend, Keith, who had offered to drive me to the race, was also tremendous in looking after me at the finish and then taking me home. How wise a move that was to have him take me to and from the event, because it seemed that all my muscles had 'locked up' after the race and I could barely move... and of course, the next morning I could not get down stairs. My wife and daughter – Doreen and Amanda, thought I was mad, and this was confirmed when I said that "for my next marathon I will train properly." This was the start of taking marathons seriously, and putting in more organised training. I began to meet a few other runners whilst out running and this gradually led to a band of comrades, and then to the birth of Hastings Runners. What wonderful early days they were, learning so much about the sport of running and enjoying our evening and morning runs.

I also missed out on the second **London Marathon** so I decided to raise monies for the British Heart Foundation by running the **Amsterdam Marathon**, a week before London. I already had contacts in Holland through the Lions Club and I was certain that it would be a flat course! Being in the potato industry, I asked all my farmers and merchants to help me raise monies by donating the value of a ton of potatoes, which was £100 at the time. They were so generous and I managed to raise over £2000. I also used the event to promote eating potatoes as good for your heart, and good for long distance races, especially the night before. The press featured me sitting amongst a ton of potatoes and I worked out that I ate about twenty-five pounds of spuds a week but was still a slim person. So much for the theory that potatoes were fattening. I ate potatoes twice a day and had a big helping the night before the marathon. I even got two Dutch potato companies to sponsor me in addition to the British Potato Marketing Board. My running T-shirts had printed on them the slogans, 'Potatoes are good for your heart' and 'Eat more potatoes.'

I felt sufficiently confident about avoiding the post race stiffness this time so drove myself to Amsterdam, taking the ferry on the morning of the event. The marathon, which started in Dam Square, was most enjoyable, with the highlights being as I approached a slight incline on the route and heard all the Dutch runners complaining about the hills!! I knew what hills were like as we have a few real ones around Hastings and could not understand the moans and groans from the other runners. I also met a wonderful Dutch runner who was 70 years old and determined to beat 3.5 hours. We stayed together for the last 6 miles and came in with a time of 3:22. This was a totally different experience from my first attempt as I felt comfortable all the way round and was probably the reason why I went on to complete five more.

However, this was not the main experience I was to remember from Amsterdam, as returning to my car I found that it had been broken into and all my clothes, money, diary and notes were gone. Fortunately, I had hidden my passport so that was still there. The Dutch police were as helpful as they could be but I was not able to contact my friends in Amsterdam as I did not have their contact details anymore. After spending most of the time at the police station, I left very early the next morning to travel back to the ferry port. As I only had my running gear and a track suit, I was overjoyed to find the ferry had a swimming pool so I spent most of the journey in the pool. Importantly, I had accomplished my main target of running a marathon within myself, by having put in the right amount of training and therefore reaping the rewards. This taught me that for marathon running, what you put in, will reflect what you get out!

These were halcyon days of running but I was determined to get into the **London Marathon** and the format for entering at that time was a system whereby designated post offices around the country would accept entries from 9am on Saturday 9th November and the first fifty entries received were guaranteed a place. Thanks to a friend who worked near the post office, who phoned me when a queue began to form around mid-afternoon on the Friday, I was able to drop everything and dash into Eastbourne in time to join the queue in eighteenth position. I spent a pleasant night outside the post office, enjoying the wonderful camaraderie of the runners who had gathered there with the same aim. I was even allowed to leave my place in the queue briefly when my wife and daughter arrived to take me out for a meal (it was my fortieth birthday). In the morning the Post Master counted the entries into the box and I was in! Strangely, I still believe to this day that this was the fairest way for dedicated runners who really wanted to take part in such an event to make sure of their entry and I think that the present system of selection is most unfair and makes it extremely difficult to obtain an entry.

I enjoyed my first **London Marathon** and finished as planned in 3:30, just when the TV cameras finished their coverage. The day had been wonderful, even though I had drunk, as was popularly advised at the time, a lot of coffee before the start and then had to stop soon afterwards to relieve myself, along with many others. I also enjoyed running with Jimmy Savile and his minders for the first time, and learned a lot from the great man in the process. What an inspiration Jimmy was to us all.

I ran another four London Marathons, with my best time of 3:12 being inspired by a female runner who will remain anonymous. It was when I was passing the 18-mile point that she called out to me and somehow I responded and found the energy to fly the last 8 miles at record pace. It's amazing what a good woman can do for you!

My wife never came to watch me as she always said that she didn't want to see me suffer but was fully supportive in all that I did. Our daughter, Amanda, did come to watch and it made all the difference to know that she would be somewhere on the route and I would be looking out for her anxiously to give her a hug and kiss, especially at 20 miles.

Every marathon runner I've spoken to has so many stories to tell of experiences during the race, and what great friendships have been forged and what fantastic characters you come across in marathon running. One person who stands out for me is a certain Lawrence Page, who had learning difficulties, but he did not allow it to stop him from running many marathons – **London, New York** and **Moscow**, making a name for himself with all these achievements. I used to enjoy our training runs together with his father, Jim, supporting him all the way. An example of one of our training runs was a 12-mile loop and often we'd get to 10 miles and Lawrence would simply say, "I've had enough, I'm going back." So we'd finish up doing 20 miles instead of the original 12! Lawrence was an example to all those with a disability as to what could be achieved.

I have had cramp before a marathon, visited most of the toilets on the **London Marathon** route, and seen the craziest starts of all in **Paris**, where runners seemed to go in all directions at the start. But my toughest was the **Seven Sisters Marathon**. This was run in February in the year I took part and I turned my ankle over early on but I was determined to keep going. The **Seven Sisters** (seven chalk sea cliffs) seemed like seventy-seven sisters in the final stages of the marathon and I recorded a finishing time of 5:35 but afterwards, relaxing in the swimming pool and enjoying the rice pudding at St Bede's, was absolute heaven.

Some of my best training runs were when I would drive to places like Brighton, Lewes, Eastbourne and Flimwell then, sometimes unwillingly, I would be forced to run back home to St Leonards on Sea while the family drove home. It was certainly one way of putting in the mileage for running a marathon... My wife announced my retirement from marathon running in the *Hastings Observer* after my best **London Marathon** time. She had had enough of unsocial meals and continual washing and ironing, and the demands of organising the Hastings Half Marathon were taking up more and more of my time. However, I still continued to enjoy the training and shorter runs.

Many athletes will have run the Hastings Half Marathon but very few will realise that the town of Hastings once organised a marathon... way back in 1908. It was when Edward VII was on the throne and Asquith had just become Prime Minister. London life was returning to normality after the Olympic Games (the one that added the now standard 385 yards to the marathon distance) had run for a record six months, and the Great War was still six years away.

It started at the Central Cricket Ground on Wednesday 16th December 1908 and fifty-one competitors took part. During the race a football match took place at the ground between Hastings United and Clapton Orient. As for the costume (running kit) every competitor had to wear complete clothing from the shoulders to the knees (i.e. jersey sleeves to the elbows and loose drawers with slips) with disqualification for any runner who was not properly attired. The main sponsor was OXO, who were also the official caterers. Competitors were supplied with an OXO flask with hot and cold OXO. Also supplied was a soda, rice pudding, raisins, bananas, milk and stimulants, with eau de cologne and sponges being carried by the OXO motors.

The objective of the event was the welfare of Hastings and the encouragement of two deserving bodies – Hastings Football Club and the Distress Committee for the relief of the Unemployed.

The winner's prize was a solid silver double-handed cup weighing 85 ounces which went to W. T. Clarke of Sefton Harriers, who clocked 2:37. A minute later came F. Lord of Wisbey Park AC in a very exhausted condition. The first Hastings man home was George White, who received the Harvey du Cross Cup. The event was a great success and also had many champions taking part.

******

Michael Martin – Seaford Striders

Marathon – what a wonderful word! And it is, as most of us know, a place in Greece (8,500 inhabitants). It's about 40 kilometres northeast of Athens, where a small force of Athenians defeated the mighty Persian army in 490 BC. The battle is famed not only for the Athenian victory against huge odds but also for the Athenian runner, Pheidippides, who was dispatched to Athens with news of the victory and fell dead from exhaustion after delivering the message to the city. Thus the name Marathon was given to long-distance running races.

Pheidippides was a professional runner, a messenger for the Athenian army. So why would a real pro drop down dead after 'only 42 km?' Well, because the 42 km was only his *pièce de résistance*, the final leg of a rather challenging ultra run. First of all, he had to run 220 km from Athens to Sparta to ask the Spartans for military support against the Persians. The Spartans agreed but because of their religious beliefs, they were not allowed to leave before the next full moon, a couple of days ahead. Unfortunately, this also applied to their own runners. So Pheidippides had to run all the way back and even further to Marathon to tell the Athenian troops that the Spartans would eventually turn up and help.

Now imagine Pheidippides' face when after approximately 480 km on arrival in Marathon he found out that the battle was already over and that the Athenians had won it anyway. But Miltiades, the Athenian leader at Marathon had another surprise for Pheidippides up his leather sleeve. He ordered him to run back to Athens to announce the glorious victory over the Persians. And so off he went again. A number of hours later he reached Athens after clocking up a total of 520 km! It's hardly surprising that he didn't survive.

I like this story even if it did end in a personal tragedy. How many times during a marathon have I felt like Pheidippides on his last legs! Maybe it's because of this historical background that I love the sound of the word 'marathon'. Yes! For some it's only a town, and yes, for others it's just the Greek word for fennel but for me 'marathon' epitomises the whole fascination of running... and not only me, it seems. That's why the name 'Marathon' has become a hugely successful global brand.

According to allaboutbranding.com, a brand is a unique and identifiable name or trademark which serves to differentiate competing products or services. Furthermore, a brand is both a physical and emotional trigger to create a relationship between consumers and the product. A physical trigger indeed. And what about emotion? Remember 2004 and Paula Radcliffe crying on the pavement in... Athens? See, there you are! Maybe she was contemplating the fate of Pheidippides in the same town nearly 2,500 years previously.

I don't think any 42 km race would be a huge success if it were not called a marathon. Even a 21 km run is marketed as a half marathon, not as a 'double 10 km and a bit' or 'Pheidippides' warm-up'. And just think of all the towns and cities where the word 'marathon' adds a little magic to their otherwise rather uninspiring names – the **Nuuk**, **Myvatin** or **Steinfurt Marathons** to name just a few.

The word 'marathon' incorporates a real promise – you have to work hard, you have to suffer, you have to do it all on your own. It will really hurt afterwards – but it will make you feel great! Just say

143

the word 'marathon' and it will melt in your mouth, it will refresh the parts that a 10 km cannot reach, it will put a tiger in your tank. Close your eyes and look at the pictures you have stored in your brain under 'marathon'... OK?... now challenge your imagination again with the words '20 mile run' or '5 km waddle' Do you feel the difference? Marathon – I'm loving it!!

******

Lorraine Kelly

Like most of us who enjoy watching the Olympics I always thought of marathon runners as almost superhuman figures, pushing themselves to the very limits of endurance – and of course, they were. But these days any reasonably fit person with decent footwear and proper training can run those 26 long miles as long as they can secure a place. I was asked to do the **London Marathon** in 2004 in aid of the British Heart Foundation. I jumped at the chance, but had no idea of what I was letting myself in for. I was very lucky to have fitness expert, Jane Wake as my trainer and she transformed me from a chubby mum into an acceptably fit woman. Jane drummed it into me and my best friend, Joyce, not to go off too fast at the start as we would use up too much energy and not be able to sustain the pace. After a sleepless night, and full of nerves, Joyce and I lined up at the so-called 'celebrity' start. I was at the front with the likes of Gordon Ramsay and Nell McAndrew who looked alarmingly fit. When the starter gun went I just wanted to run like the wind but I could hear Jane's voice in my head telling me to take it easy, and so I slowed down and let all the pumped up and much more fit runners zoom past.

We did pretty well, Joyce and I, for a couple of 45-year-olds. We kept each other going and talked about everything under the sun. At one point we were overtaken by a couple of Cornish pasties and that was a bit soul destroying but we weren't there to break any records, we just wanted to finish.

In the end, it took us over 5 hours, and we were utterly exhausted at the finish, but crossing the line and giving my daughter, Rosie, a big hug was fantastic. I did it all over again in 2005, but I wasn't as fit and it took us a bit longer, but the camaraderie, the crowd, the atmosphere and the sheer joy of crossing the line were just the same. Later in November 2005, Joyce and I did the **New York Marathon** and that was just awesome (as the Yanks say). I suffered from blisters and bruised toenails for the first time and was pretty shattered, especially as after I crossed the line at around 5pm I had to stay up until two in the morning to do a live link from New York to GMTV and then just jump straight on the plane home.

It was a wonderful experience but it did take a lot out of me although along with the team from Highland Spring we managed to raise £200,000 for Breast Cancer Care which was well worth my big toenail turning black and falling off.

I think I have hung up my running shoes now, but I still do the Moonwalk in aid of breast cancer. It is a 26 mile walk at midnight wearing a decorated bra and involves about 15,000 women and some men in London in May and 8,000 people in Edinburgh in June. I am glad that I ran the marathon and think I proved to myself that I can rise to the challenge and that I am not a quitter – but never underestimate those miles!

******

Hugh Graham

The author of this book and I were students together back in the late 60s at King Alfred's College of Education, Winchester. We knew each other vaguely but had different interests and different friendship groups. There was naturally some overlap but we eventually went our separate ways having completed our respective courses and for my part, running was not a feature of my life. I played rugby, and running was seen only as a necessary evil to be endured as part of the training regime which was demanded of us. My teaching career encompassed games lessons and I was probably reasonably fit but never exceptionally so. I have never been small and my build and gait were never really meant for running but I enjoyed what little I did.

In 1981 I joined the Health Education Council on a secondment from school and became part of a national organisation dedicated to promoting fitness. I started to work harder at my running and noticed that my rugby improved at the same time. When I took up a senior management post in Sussex in 1984, the running boom was well underway and Martin Bulger's name kept appearing in the frame. I managed to get round the **London Marathon** in 1988 in 4:40, participated in numerous shorter distances in the following years and volunteered as a marshal for the **Seven Sisters Marathon**, whose start was close to my home.

When I heard that Les Smith and Tony Raven, who had organised the **Seven Sisters Marathon** for years, were to retire, I felt that I had to do something to save the event. It had a worldwide reputation as a personal challenge to all who got round the gruelling course and Eastbourne could ill-afford to lose an event of such stature. So I produced a business case for Eastbourne Borough Council to take up the reins and, with my colleague Nicola Williams in tow, have been the organiser ever since then. Some rebranding was necessary at the outset and the **Beachy Head Marathon** was launched in 2002 and has since gone from strength to strength.

These days I run to maintain fitness but an arthroscopy means that the distances are much shorter. However, each year I say to people that I run the **Beachy Head Marathon** and it's true, I do... but only as the event manager. I have great pleasure in showcasing one of the most popular marathons in the Country and have to say that it has been a privilege to play a part in marathon running from an organisational perspective.

******

Amanda Wilkins

I was never an athlete. My sport at school was tennis, something that I played at every opportunity. When Sir Bob Geldof organised his original 'Run the World' the thought of running in an event that was being held at exactly the same time all over the world appealed to me. I went down to Preston Park in Brighton and entered the 1-mile event but when I passed the finishing post I felt so fresh that I decided to continue and complete the 6-mile challenge. That gave me the taste for running and I started doing 10 km races. These proved to be too fast for the pace that I wanted to run at, so when someone suggested I try longer distance races, I took their advice and entered the Windsor Great Park Half Marathon. I thoroughly enjoyed it and it has become my favourite distance. I always enjoyed watching the **London Marathon** and decided that I ought to do it one day but when I entered the 1989 event and was accepted, I panicked. I went to the Withdean Stadium gym in Brighton and asked for help and the staff there worked out a training programme and even monitored my diet.

I trained really hard and when the race approached, I went to London with my mother for three days. At the marathon exhibition I met Steve Cram who gave me great encouragement then, staying at the same hotel as us in Victoria, were members of the Sheffield Wednesday football team who were raising money for the Hillsborough disaster. They invited me to join them for breakfast and, throughout the marathon, kept a caring eye on me.

I found it really exciting. Children lined the route, offering us sweets, and someone at the Docklands Railway gave me a cap. It took me 6:04 but I felt like a champion. I had run much further than I'd ever run before and had a fantastic time. I have done the London Marathon twice more since; my best time being in 1992 when I recorded 4:40. The following year I notched up another 'highlight' when I took second prize in my age category in the tough Hastings Half Marathon.

Marathon running then disappeared from my life until 2003 when at the age of 59 I completed the gruelling **Beachy Head Marathon** (formerly the **Seven Sisters Marathon**). My training had not been very good so I entered as a walker but still found it very tough. It took me 9 hours 30 minutes and I finished by torchlight. When I saw Eastbourne Pier all lit up from the top of Beachy Head I burst into tears!!

Now, three years on I have set my sights on doing the New York in 2007, a month before my sixty-third birthday. That will be my fourth marathon and I have heard that the more marathons you do, the more you'll want to do, but I have never professed to be a runner. I am a jogger who does it for fun and to raise money for charity. Some runners disapprove of this but I never enter an event that has a time limit, and I always start at the back – I know my place!

*****

Kay McDonald – Seaford Striders

Although as a PE student I was reasonably fit, running wasn't my 'thing' and I only really started running because of karate. We trained three times a week and part of that training was running, probably for stamina building, unless of course it was to practise the ultimate means of defence – running away!

I trained on my own and entered my first fun run – the Tunbridge Wells 10.6 miles race in 1982. I had no idea how to train properly and was ill-prepared but I did complete it and importantly, enjoyed the experience. I then joined Tunbridge Wells Runners and decided to train for the marathon. I say 'the' and not 'a' marathon because I had only ever heard of the **London Marathon** so I applied for the 1984 event and luckily, was accepted. Once again, my training felt inadequate, not having run more than 16 miles but I did finish, which I suppose is the aim of every first timer. I clocked 5:06 and like most runners doing their first marathon, I was awestruck by the incredible atmosphere – from queuing up to register on the Saturday morning along with other runners of all nationalities, and seeing the crowds of people lining the streets of the capital, to crossing the finishing line on Westminster bridge it was all just phenomenal. I was truly bitten! and also convinced that I could do better. I was lucky enough to be accepted for the **London Marathon** in 1985 and having a degree of experience this time, I managed to run all the way and record a finishing time of 4:05, reducing my PB by more than an hour… But of course now, being so close, I wanted to break 4 hours and so, marathon number three beckoned.

Meanwhile, I had met Andy, my husband-to-be. He had never run before. His sport was golf and, whilst at school, basketball. At six feet three inches tall, not only did that suit his love of basketball but it also empowered him with a long and seemingly effortless stride which was ideal for running. We did most of our courting 'on the hoof' and he entered his first race in 1986, a 10 km at Yalding. I realised I was outrun when I saw him disappear into the distance in that race. We married in September of 1986 and moved to Seaford. There we met Martin Bulger who had decided to see if there was any interest in the town for the forming of a running club. Andy became one of the founder members of the club and is still going strong with the club 20 years later. In 1987 in **Paris** I ran my third marathon and Andy joined me to run his first. He finished unchivalrously just in front of me in 4:05 with me clocking 4:07. It was an amazing experience running round Paris, the only problems with this event being the lack of toilet facilities at the beginning and that runners had to get to the half way point within 2.5 hours otherwise they were pulled out. It certainly made for a tense first half for one section of the runners.

The following year saw us return to the **London Marathon** and, while I was slower at 4:15, Andy was getting faster, 4:01 this time. My running career was then put on hold whilst I had two children and Andy continued to run and managed a creditable 3:45 in 1991. Each time one or both of us ran London, the atmosphere was always almost indescribable – the crowd support, the camaraderie among the runners, the euphoria of finishing, the pain of recovery and the absolute certainty of me saying that I will never try to run another marathon ever again... but then I discovered cross-country marathons, in particular, my favourite – the **Seven Sisters** – which I have now completed five times. I have also run the **Neolithic Marathon** in Wiltshire and a couple more 'Londons' but I keep coming back to what is for me a local event, now renamed the **Beachy Head Marathon**. A more challenging course I cannot imagine, unless you go into the mountains, with the last 7 miles of the marathon going along the cliffs of the Seven Sisters then Beachy Head itself and finally a steep drop down into Eastbourne. I cannot run all the way (most people can't) so I don't feel pressurised to do so. I see it as a 'fun' day out over local hills. Both Andy and I intend 'running' it this year. Me, to celebrate my fiftieth birthday, which falls on the very day and Andy (his tenth marathon) because it just seems like a good idea for us. Running has become a way of life, a lovely way of life, and although I do not train as much as I used to because of other commitments and injuries getting in the way, I do more cycling instead now as I feel I do not recover as quickly from marathons as I used to and yet, I still get drawn back to the call of running, and having completed thirteen marathons so far, I shall thoroughly enjoy celebrating this year's **Beachy Head Marathon**... and after I finish and I'm going through the aches and pain barrier, will it be my last marathon?... probably not.

******

Jenny Mills – Launceston Road Runners

What made me start running? I suppose that it was always needing to be very energetic... and isn't running just perfect? You don't need to find a team, a court, pitch, partner, ball, water, expensive gear or any tuition. Mankind was constructed specially for running. First of all to catch his dinner and then later in his evolution, for fun and simple exercise. So why do I run marathons? (that's fifty-five so far) well, because they're fun of course – aren't they? Then there's always a sense of adventure in participating in a marathon, often heightened by the weather conditions. For instance, it snowed one year on the **Cornish Marathon**, which was tough because there's not much shelter up on Bodmin Moor. I cooked in the intense heat on the **Greenway** at Stratford-upon-Avon and ran all 26.2 miles of the **Neolithic Marathon** into a wicked head-on gale.

I would be dishonest if I didn't also include the thrill of the competitive side of races. I'm extremely fortunate in that for my age-group (FV55) I seem to achieve reasonable success, my best time being 3:27 at **Taunton** 2006.

I enjoy too, the camaraderie, the variety of scenery and the experience of running different marathons, such as the **Isle of Man**, which is a small event with superb food and great organisation, and is almost traffic-free. As for the **Tresco Marathon** (which has no traffic) I enjoyed an amazing weekend there, running through unbelievable scenery straight out of the brochures. And then there was the **Longford Marathon** in the Republic of Ireland which is run in August. It's hot, open and flat but made special by the wonderful Irish informality and hospitality.

Incidentally, my most hated thing in running has to be runners who discard bottles, gel wrappers, banana skins and sponges at the furthest point from the drinks station instead of throwing them in at the next one. What I like most however, is the way we all support each other and just enjoy 'being there, running it.'

******

Bob & Jane Webster – Seaford Striders

Jane: I hated all sports at school, even running. Whether that was due to a natural aversion to exercise or just not getting on very well with the PE teachers, I'm not sure. However, when I married Bob, who had already done over 200 marathons I suppose I must have realised that it was only a matter of time before I would do my first. Making the transition from marathon widow to marathon runner (gamekeeper to poacher... or is it the other way round?) was not easy but with Bob's encouragement I decided to have a go. The **Rottingdean Marathon** was quickly followed by the 2003 **Isle of Man** Grand Prix and despite declaring "never again" I did eventually resume training once more.

I had been supporting Bob over a cross-country event and thought that it would be fun having to use 'route instructions' to guide you, and in doing so, seeing parts of the country not normally viewed from a car or on short walks. That was in 2004 and since then 'the flood gates have opened' for both marathons and ultras. I don't appear to have a problem with stamina but blisters and a weak right shoulder, particularly on ultras, are my downfall.

The **Black Mountains Roundabout** and the **Snowdon Marathon** have very quickly become my favourites. In the case of the BMR I think it is pure madness to drag oneself up sides of mountains in the fog trying to find checkpoints and wading a foot deep in bogs but there is a seriousness to the event which I enjoy. Then there is the fun of getting back down the other side – perhaps this is the mountain goat in me, my zodiac sign being Capricorn.

The **Snowdon** run on the road is probably the easiest event I do, the miles just seem to fly by, the drinks stations are plentiful, the scenery wonderful, the support from the roadside is friendly and noisy and the cup of hot, sweet tea at the top of the mountain is the best cuppa I have all year. And then I have the joy of overtaking some of

151

the ones who overtook me on the way up (and the flat) because they do not have the goat's nimbleness on the way down. It could be just a coincidence that my two favourites are both in Wales or maybe it's due to a hereditary instinct – some of my forbears having come from Wales.

My bogey event is the **Isle of Man Marathon**, and if it were not for the fact that I love the place and holiday there each year, I would not recommend it. The event is on road and not particularly hard but it's still a slog due to the weather usually being very warm and muggy. It has the added bête-noire of being a two-lap course – for me there is nothing worse than having to go round again... And it doesn't seem to matter how much I train beforehand, I crawl round! However, the marathon is part of the island's Grand Prix week and is followed by four short races, on various evenings – too fast for me but boy, do I love the climb up Peel Hill on the Monday and Friday, if only for the chance to put my mountain goat skills to the test.

I continue to be slow – frustratingly so – often being accompanied by the sweeper – a subject which alone could fill a book alone – and this in itself often has me wanting to throw the towel in. So why don't I? I don't know. My mother would love it if I did. She knows, she simply knows, that Bob is forcing me round 26.2 miles. But I reply to her, "Mum, you cannot make someone run a marathon if they don't want to." And she'd respond with "but you never liked sport at school." But as the guy at the recent Northumberland 100 said: "it's not like other sports... It's self-challenging!" And I suppose that's where it's just as hard for the front runners as it is for me. They are all trying to be first while I'm trying just as hard not to be last! But in any event, who in their right mind staggers round in freezing cold rain and snow, gale force winds and 90 degrees of heat, not to mention up to their kneecaps in peat bogs.

Two things stop me from giving up. One is the thought of going through all the agony of training from the beginning again. Secondly, and this is what I always say when asked, marathons are like having a baby – one soon forgets the pain... Oh, and thirdly, Bob won't let me.

Bob: I started running at school, mainly cross country as they thought I was too slow for anything else. I am in the Alf Tupper/sweeper class, but slow and steady wins the race. Our daughter India, often gets in on the act. I have not quite carried her for a full marathon yet but being out for 16 miles with her is almost in that category!

As regards road events, I have always been very cavalier. I believe that, in our sport, enjoying it must always be paramount. I just love the off-road events, not particularly for the scenery any more (been there, done that, etc) I guess I am just addicted to 1:50,000 Landranger Maps and Silva compasses. A marathon is often called a 'race' but for me, the race starts when you have gone through 39 miles. The race against attrition! Will my body stand up to it? Sometimes I find myself comparing marathons, musing on their differences, my likes and dislikes, for instance, at the Isle of Man Marathon in August 2006, shortly before the start: "You got a bad leg Bob?" asked a fellow centurion.

"It's only sore when I walk on it and I haven't taken pain killers," I replied.

"Will you be able to get round though?" he continued.

"Well, it's only 26.2 miles and it's only the Isle of Man," was my reply...

To be quite honest, I wasn't just in pain, I was in agony, because six weeks earlier on the **Tanners Marathon** I had landed heavily. Now, with the aid of leg supports and pain killers I could get around under my own steam... but only just! Maybe, just maybe, trying for a good time in the Downland 30, three weeks previously, had been a bit too soon after the 'Tanners' to try for my 'comeback'. I had rested last weekend but it hurt even more to miss the Caerphilly Summits than the pain in my leg. But this was only the **Isle of Man Marathon**. Take out Bride Hill and you are left with a flat run. I knew I could shuffle round even with my leg as it was. I admit the first mile along Ramsey prom wasn't too comfortable, but as I ran past the Island Hotel on the cliff road I settled into a routine. By the time I did Bride Hill for the first time I was comfortable from a mixture of painkillers, rhythm and my MP3 player.

There were cheers from the checkpoint staff, round the corner and a steady descent to Andreas followed by an almost flat section to St Jude's then down the valley and back to Ramsey. Hold it together going past Ballacloan Stadium (the finishing venue) then a steadier run up the prom, with no one expecting me to try sprinting this time. Then, all I had to do was to 'find' Bride Hill again and see the second lap through. Yes, I was the last one in! Yes, I did take 6 hours 29 minutes! and true, my leg was throbbing... but importantly, for me, I had clocked another marathon. Enjoy your Manx holidays if you want. I come to run... and run I did! However, the official organiser came to ask me if I had walked it. To say I was a bit deflated, not to say, upset, was a bit of an understatement! The cuppa at the finish was nice though... but I still haven't found it in me to wear the T-shirt yet.

My experience of the **Isle of Wight** three months earlier was entirely different. It was only six days before the LDWA Northumberland 100, with the **Cornish Marathon** still only a dream on the horizon. I had loosened up for it with a steady run at Marlborough the day before, where the mud was only ankle deep and the Downs only a bit steep but the post race cuppa had fortified me!

Over a period of three weeks before the **Isle of Wight** I had done two 40-miler races and four of just 35 miles or less. The IOW is of course, a mere 26.2 miles but as far as I'm concerned, it is about the second hardest road marathon and nothing like you come across off-road. However, the previous day's Marlborough event had left me feeling jaded, although having said that I always feel that I don't properly settle into the **Isle of Wight Marathon** until I've cleared Newport. That's when I really start to enjoy the event. The hills may be a bit steep, Godshill a bit touristy and going past the donkey sanctuary a bit of a slog, but the 'reward' comes on the stretch through Shanklin, Lake and Sandown. I always find Brading a bit of a challenge, though I do look forward to it, just as I do the hill at 23 miles leading to the old Isle of Wight airport, now Tescos and McDonalds. The final descent of about a mile I tend to find a bit painful but my mind makes comparisons with the downhill into Pensilva on the **Cornish Marathon** and I am still in some sort of heaven. The final run-in round the boating/paddling pool, with the end in sight reminds me that the end of yet another Isle of Wight experience is approaching. As luck would have it, I managed to get a cuppa afterwards from the mother and son team who run the café close by, thus making the whole day worthwhile.

Later that year I ran the 'Snowdonia' then, with a three-week break, ran the **Cornish Marathon**. Now I see that as doing the easiest marathon in the world followed by the hardest. Nothing in my mind can be easier than that nice stroll up Llanberis Pass followed by a nice 9 miles steadily downhill to Beddgelert, then 8 miles of easy undulations to Waunfawr, with 2 miles uphill, a mile flat, ending with a 2-mile descent to the finish. All this with every Army cadet in Gwynedd wanting to ply you with all the drink and food and cheers you can hope for on the way round, with a nice cuppa from the Welsh National Trust ladies as a reward at the finish.

Fast forward 3 weeks to the **Cornish Marathon** and I'm at 13 miles on Bodmin Moor, running through the frozen gap between Colliford Reservoir and Dozymary Pool. No support, just a lonely drag to Jamaica Inn two miles further on, and I can't believe I've only done 15 miles. I'm not quite frozen but my mind is wondering how cold the Fowey Valley is going to be for the next 8 miles… It was freezing! I start to climb the Cornish Wall at 21 miles. The Guides give me good cheer and at 24 miles I enter Higher Tremarcombe. I think that every Guide in Caradon is at the drinks table supporting the runners. At the Crow's nest, I'm crawling home with only 1.5 miles to go and it seems like I am re-climbing the Cornish Wall. I blink and miss a smidgen of downhill before yet another climb to the crest. The half-mile to the end must be the only downhill which makes you feel as though you are climbing the American North-West ridge on Everest. I pass 26 miles and it seem like the 385 yards still to go is like 385 miles. I can see the finish. I am swinging in. Have I only really been running for 5 hours 51 minutes…? Where's that cup of tea?

******

155

Debbie Pentlands – Portsmouth Joggers

Fourteen years ago I was diagnosed with Systemic Lupus Erythematosus (SLE). It is an auto-immune disease that affects the whole body, from your skin to your internal organs, causing all kinds of problems, from rashes to inflammation around the joints and internal organs and even the brain. I was told that there was no cure but it could be controlled with medication. However, even with the six different drugs I was on, I was still a wreck. I would work and sleep. My husband Bob would wake me up to feed me and I would go back to sleep again. This went on for around six years and I felt shattered all the time. So I decided to read all I could on exercise, diet, alternative therapy and alternative medicine.

I read and read everything I could get my hands on. I tried all the alternative therapies from massage, reiki and Indian Head, to shiatsu, yoga, tai chi and Pilates. I changed my diet for the better, eating as much fruit and veg and food in its natural state as I could. I joined the Optimum Nutrition Association in London and I slowly but surely began to feel better. One of the drugs I was on, was prednisolone, a steroid. I knew, however, that these destroyed bone density so I thought that if I joined the gym and started to do a wee bit of jogging it would all help to build my bones and hopefully combat the adverse side effect of the drug.

I finally managed to get up to a half mile run non-stop and, encouraged by a runner in our gym, I gradually (after about three months) had increased the distance to 3 miles. I couldn't believe it. I could run for 30 minutes non-stop. I was on cloud nine! Then, one day the gym was so busy that I decided to do my run outside. I ran along Southsea seafront, enjoying the fresh air, the sound of the waves and even the seagulls. It was wonderful. When I got back I was grinning from ear to ear, and my runner friend asked me where I had gone to. When I told him where I had run, he smiled, and informed me that I had run FIVE miles. I was amazed and felt absolutely chuffed to bits.

From there, I steadily progressed from five miles to five **London Marathons** and one **Beachy Head Marathon**. Bob and I run three or four times a week and always have a race on Sundays.

Slowly, over the eight and a half years since I started running I have come off all the drugs and although the Lupus is still there and it gets me on the odd occasion, I keep pretty well. I now teach exercise for a living, teaching people in the 50+ age range tai chi, various exercises to music and do a lot of work with the Social Services Falls Prevention Team, working in conjunction with our local hospital physiotherapy department. It's strange to think, that if it had not been for me getting Lupus I would not be a runner today. So you have to be positive and make the best of any situation. You never know what might happen.

******

Richard & Jacqui Walker – Hout Bay Harriers

Jacqui had been running for a few years with a couple of half marathons under her belt whilst living in York and my exploits were limited to a few 10 km races in my late twenties. Then in 1998 Jacqui and I moved with the family to South Africa. Jacqui joined the Hout Bay Harriers, which is a club just outside Cape Town. She joined the 5.45 a.m. group running approximately three times a week and entered races up to the half marathon distance. In 1999 due to my expanding waistline, thanks to beer and braais (that's South African for barbeques) I took up walking but soon got bored so I decided to run as the pain was over more quickly and eventually I joined the same running group as Jacqui. Hout Bay Harriers were easily recognised by their trademark pink shorts – great for the ladies but character building for the men!!! The bug really took hold over both of us and we found ourselves training five or six times a week. In addition, we entered races every other week. The decision to run a marathon was an inevitable consequence of the running we were doing and the enjoyment that we were getting from both the countryside we were running through and the camaraderie of our fellow runners. Our first marathon was the 1999 **Cape Town City Marathon** – a truly dreadful experience for both of us despite all the hours of training and preparation. Every kilometre after the 25 km mark seemed like an eternity. However, reassured by our running colleagues at the Club that the first was always the worst, we entered more, including the blue ribbon event in the Cape Town area – the **Two Oceans Marathon** – consisting of 56 km (therefore an ultra marathon) with a cut-off time of 7 hours. Jacqui and I did two of these and the one that sticks in the mind was the second one, when both of us hobbled over the line before the cut-off suffering with iliotibial band (Jacqui) and hamstring (me) injuries. Some would call it stupid as both injuries flared up around the 7 km mark but the atmosphere was brilliant and we just got swept along with the 10,000 or so other competitors. A couple of massages along the way also helped. One other (of our nine marathons) that sticks in the mind was the **Cango Caves Marathon** at Oudsthoorn, near George in the Western Cape, an area noted for breeding ostriches. We both completed the standard marathon course in less than 4 hours but the heat was incredible, finishing just before 10am with the temperature approaching 40°C. Water stops were situated every kilometre for the last 10 km and we can both recall taking on about five sachets each at every station – down the hatch, over the head, on the face and down the back etc. Jacqui did wonderfully well between 1999 and 2004, regularly finishing in the top five of the running clubs women's section. I cannot ever recall finishing in front of Jacqui so I saw plenty of her backside. Being a plodder does have its compensations!

Running has brought us closer together – having shared interests. We've relished the battles against the elements and conquering the 'wall' and all the self doubt. We have certainly enjoyed the competitiveness and clocking up PBs but most important of all was the camaraderie.

Since returning from South Africa in 2005 running has had to take a back seat due to our work commitments but we sincerely hope that we can replicate those wonderful running years at some time in the near future.

******

Karen Bowler – Hailsham Harriers

I started running when Tim, my husband, joined the local rugby club when we first moved to Sussex in the early 80s. I was jealous that he was making friends while I was stuck at home renovating the place. So one day I put on my trainers and ran round Tim's training route. When I told him, he didn't believe I could run 3 miles without stopping so he accompanied me the next time. At the halfway point I decided to increase my speed and finished well ahead of Tim. He was quite surprised and impressed by my pace so he registered me to run the Eastbourne 10-mile event the following weekend. I completed it so comfortably that I decided to enter the **London Marathon** the next year and followed that by entering the **Harlow Marathon**. In that race I was the first female to finish and, with a time of 3:10 qualified for the British Championships held within the 1983 **London Marathon**.

Although I have been lucky enough to have won championship gold medals at 20 miles, 25 km, 10 km and 1500 metres, the achievement that I rate as my best was winning the 1985 Welsh Marathon Championship.

I run because I enjoy it, especially when I'm running well, and if I could rerun the last 25 years, the only thing I'd change would be to find someone to train me.

******

Alex Parsons – Seaford Striders

I started running in the summer of 2005 because Nick, now my husband, loved running, and I wanted to get fit and lose a few pounds. I thought I was reasonably fit from scuba diving and swimming but I had never run before, not even to catch a bus. Running was simply alien to me and running with Nick was tough as he's a real hard task master who has been running 10 kms and half marathons for quite a long while, and thought that walking was giving up! He got me started, but after a month or so I realised it was time to find running buddies of my level. A great diving friend introduced me to the

Seaford Striders and that is where my new found challenges really began.

The people at the Running Club were fantastic – not too soft and not too pushy. There is a competitive edge which encourages everyone to perform to the best of their ability, but there's really only one person to beat, and only one person to do it – and that's yourself.

My first race was a 5-miler cross-country event in Abbott's Wood, just north of Eastbourne. It may not be everyone's ideal first race but it suited me well. Running towards the back of the field meant that by the time I began the second lap of the course, the surface, that seemed to be predominantly clay had been well and truly churned up, turning it into a thick, leg-grabbing, energy-sapping, squelchy mud that was awash with rivers that weren't there in the first lap. Not only that, but we also waded through a river almost up to the waist. I loved every minute of it, and continued to enter races after that baptism of mud. I have never been much of a spectator and Nick was back into running so it was either take part and burn some calories or watch and get cold. The choice was easy – join in!

In July 2006 Nick and I got married. As our special day approached, we were busy and getting very excited. One of my bridesmaids told me that after your wedding there can be a big anticlimax so it's a good idea to plan something exciting a few months later… Most of the Seaford Striders seem to have done at least one marathon and three of them have done hundreds. It is quite normal in the club for someone to be going off somewhere to do a marathon at any time of the year. As a result, I had found the 'something' to combat the after-wedding blues…. I would enter the **Beachy Head Marathon**!!! The training was tough but a veteran of many Beachy Head Marathons also decided to enter and help us to train for the big day. We all trained together and I thought my lack of experience would hold up the others but to my surprise, it didn't. Nick was impressed with how quickly I had been able to increase my speed and distance over the past few months and he was also realising now that he had a lot to learn – about walking! No more non-stop road running because this was different. We were learning how to pace oneself for 26.2 miles over the South Downs, as no way could you run up every hill and expect to have the energy to complete the course. After all, we had three months to train not three years.

We soon learned how slowly we needed to run, which hills to walk up and which ones to run. The weeks passed and the miles clocked up. Three weeks before the big day was our longest run, 21 miles... and at the end... wow! we all felt great. We were ready but for just a few warm down races – a couple of 10 milers and some recovery time. Oh how those last three weeks dragged. I think I had become hooked on our early morning runs over the Downs but now there was a sense of feeling cheated out of the enjoyment of long runs.

The week before was so exciting. In diving (my other love) you are taught to plan the dive and dive the plan. This is what I knew. I was running on my own so I aimed to plan the run to run the plan. This was my strategy and my coping tool. I bought a running belt for my jelly babies... well, it's not often you can eat as much as you like as often as you like and get away with it, and a disposable camera because I was only going to do one marathon. Entering the marathon was a moment of madness and I may as well have photographic evidence of it.

The day loomed and the days of drinking water and eating bread, potatoes and pasta were becoming very dull and what I really wanted was a nice glass of wine with our penultimate meal of pasta. So, early to bed it was. I can't imagine why, but it was one of the most restless nights' sleep I have ever had. Maybe I was dreaming about that first hill, the West Dean steps or the Seven Sisters – I have no idea. However, by 5am we were eating our 'last supper' of porridge and pints of water. Then we were off. The roads to Eastbourne were so busy that early in the morning. Are there really that many people taking part in this marathon? Yes, 1,750 of us. By 7 a.m. we were parking just outside St Bedes School and looking up at 'that first hill'. The other competitors in the school at that time looked very skinny, serious muscled fell runners... then there was me! Luckily, our other Seaford Strider buddies soon turned up which made me feel far less out of place. 8:30 a.m. – my last trip to the loo. Vaseline and Deep Heat on, a last Jaffa cake and a swig of energy drink, fill up the water bottle and load the jelly babies... then it's off to the start. We'd arrived at the school in plenty of time – 2 hours in fact, with all the

161

time in the world yet it still seemed like a mad panic in the last half hour... strange!

Wow! There are 1,750 people clad in vests, shorts and trainers on a cold overcast October morning, all looking at the big steep hill. People are standing at the top with cameras poised ready to get that action shot, maybe someone will run this hill. Bang, bang, the maroons are let off and the marathon gets under way... mostly at a brisk walking pace, which has to be the slowest race start ever. This is tortoise racing... I like this. At the top of the hill is the most amazing view of Eastbourne Bay. It really is beautiful and I hope to be looking at that view again in about five and a half hours' time.

The first few miles are wonderful. The piper is playing the bagpipes on top of the hill and we all start to run over the Downs into a slightly misty horizon. At this point I decide not to take photos. This place and time is magic... I will do it again. I now know that it was not a moment of madness but a moment of sanity.

Down, down in to Jevington, and my mother and father are there with supplies of water and more jelly babies. Yummy, I can eat lots today. Off we go again, back up another rutty chalk path, there's a walker with two sticks whizzing past all us runners... must follow him... must stop eating jelly babies and walk with a mission... mission accomplished.

The miles pass by and soon I'm running on my well-trodden training ground. Up on the Downs the wind is strong but refreshing. I keep one eye on my plan and I reach each checkpoint at the planned times, then arrive at 'High and Over' where the Seaford Striders are manning the road crossing. It's really nice to see familiar faces, so a quick hello and then it's down through the Cuckmere Valley to Litlington, the checkpoint renowned for the amazing food. I'm really looking forward to this but I don't seem to be able to eat anything. Typical! The one day you can eat and eat... and I don't feel like it. I know the next few miles will be tough. There are two lots of steps to climb but other Seaford Striders appear from nowhere so we climb them together. But the best is yet to come (or the worst, depending on how tired you are) It used to be called the **Seven Sisters Marathon** for a very good reason – seven, well actually eight, steep rollercoaster hills crammed into 2 miles.

At the Cuckmere estuary I refilled my water bottle. That sounds ambiguous. What I actually mean is… oh never mind. I glance up at the start of the Seven Sisters and note that it has taken me 3 hours and 55 minutes to cover 20 miles of the South Downs… only 6 miles to go. Can I finish in less than five and half hours? It's worth a go, but those hills really are very steep… and who put those lumps of chalk in the way? They hurt my feet. I join forces with a fellow runner who tells me all about her children as we walk up and run down the Sisters. On the fourth Sister I see a mirage – the Coastguard Landrover is on top of the hill manning a water station…. So nice to see him… an excuse to stop for a few minutes.

The last two Sisters lead to Birling Gap but its only 3 miles to go and if I push on I might make that five and a half hour finish so I don't stop. 2 hills to go… or so I thought. Two hills later and there's still one to go… I'm sure that it wasn't there before. From the top of the hill, the last and final hill (Beachy Head) is that amazing view of Eastbourne. I know it's all down hill now… and out of nowhere, my legs start to run faster and faster… I'm on autopilot… Number 977 finishes in 5 hours 40 minutes. That's me… When can I do it again?

******

Glynis Young – Seaford Striders

Way back in 1987 I was a housewife and mother who had three children and a part time job. My husband, who was in the Royal Navy, was away for long periods and in my spare time I ran a Girl Guide Company. So why did I take up running? The Guide Company that I ran belonged to an Area which had the opportunity to buy a piece of land, suitable for a campsite. Obviously, we needed to raise money to buy the land and equip the site so a close friend of mine suggested that as I was a 'fit' person, I ought to run the local 10 km race and get some sponsorship. What a good idea!! So, on a gloriously sunny day in June, after a couple of months training (I use the term 'training' loosely here) I donned my green flash plimsolls and lined up at the start. I managed the steep hill, the humid pathway between hedges and the very long, slow hill just after the halfway point. However, just as I crossed the finishing line I was struck with one almighty disabling migraine. It was so bad that I could not get home without help and when I did I went to bed for the rest of the day. I was most upset because I had been looking forward to a plate of fish and chips after all my hard work. This meal was going to be a big treat as I had been on a strict weight-loss diet as part of my training... wrong!! At the time, I didn't know about carbo loading, energy drinks or fitness diets. Anyway, I took so much ribbing and criticism from my family and friends that I decided to do another run. I just wanted to prove to my worst critics that I was fit, but a migraine sufferer, so it was not the running which made me ill.

I found out that my next local run was a 10-mile event so I resumed my training. It went well, the diet was a success and so was the run. In fact I was particularly pleased with my efforts because I had managed to pass a couple from the local running club... how good was that!! I was still reflecting on my triumphant run when my daughter came home from school and said – "my teacher, Martin Bulger, wondered if you would like to join the running club." I must have done well.

I went along to the club and met the runners – what a nice lot!! Two members took me out for a training run and they talked the whole time while I only just managed to keep up with their pace. Words could not pass my lips as I was so intent on trying to breathe. From then on, training took on another meaning. The green flash plimsolls were traded in for a proper pair of running shoes, new 'minimal' bounce underwear was purchased and tracksters were obtained. I was hooked.

Running became a big part of my life. I was much fitter and slimmer as I was now eating all the right food. I was much happier and life seemed so much better. I had just one 'couch potato' left who criticised my running but I knew that I could rise above any comments and enjoy my running and myself. Having learned how to run and having joined the Seaford Striders, I found myself having so much fun that I wanted to do more. One of the club members suggested I try the Hastings Half Marathon as she thought I was now capable of the distance and she also offered to run it with me. We trained very hard and even though I suffered badly with a cold and chest infection beforehand I managed to make it to the start line. This was not only the longest run but also the biggest event I had ever taken part in. So, on my thirty-ninth birthday, which was also Mothering Sunday, I completed my first half marathon. As we crossed the finishing line I asked my running partner if we had managed a good time. She replied that it was a PB for her and so we were both very pleased with our efforts. Another surprise at the finish was seeing all my children. They had planned to be at the finish as it was such a special day for me, and they even produced a bottle of bubbly and some glasses.

Later on in the year I was asked if I felt up to doing the marathon distance. If I did, I was told that the London Marathon entry forms were available and I should fill one in and try for a place. Sadly, I was rejected. My fellow club mates tried to get me to enter other marathons but I said I would like London to be my first marathon, just in case it was my first and last one. Five years later I managed to secure a place in the **London Marathon**... but that is another story.

When asked "why run marathons?" I reply, "because they are there and because they are fun!" My marathon running career lasted for thirty events until, unfortunately, osteoarthritis crept into my knee joints so I only had a limited time to take part in these great runs. I could tell you about the local cross-country marathons and about the year I ran marathons as part of my training for the South Downs 80-mile event but I won't. Instead, I would just like to recount my favourite marathon – LONDON.

My very first marathon, for which I had waited five years to get a place, was at London. I had seen it on television and wanted to go and have some fun like the thousands of runners I'd seen. I decided to make it fun by wearing a fancy dress costume and as I was raising money for Guy's Hospital I decided to run as a nurse. I had managed quite a bit of training so I was determined to try for a good time too. To sharpen my resolve my running partner said she would double the money she had sponsored me for if I ran under four and a half hours. Another runner from the club became my other running partner and the three of us started the hardest amount of training I had ever thought possible. (Nothing like Paula's 150 miles a week).

Everything went well and I was ready and well prepared for the big day. At 6 a.m. on the morning of the Marathon I joined my fellow club mates on a coach to London. I remember it was a crisp, frosty morning, I had missed my alarm and it was a friend, who was also running, who thankfully woke me just in time for me to get to the coach. On arriving in London we left the coach near the Royal Naval College to walk up through Greenwich Park to the start. That year there were about 32,000 people running and as I walked through the park, in awe of the 'millions' of people who were there, to my utmost amazement I found myself walking alongside my brother. I knew he had intended running as his firm were sponsoring the **London Marathon** that year but I never expected to see him, especially with so many runners, spectators and supporters milling around at the start. After depositing my kit bag on the baggage lorries I went excitedly to the start line. I must admit that I am one of very many people who get a lump in the throat and a tear in the eye when the cannon is fired and the music starts to play.

My costume was a hit with the spectators and I think the cheers and calls of encouragement to 'nurse', 'sister' and 'matron' kept me going. I found the crowd amazing and missed them when I reached the area near the Isle of Dogs. It was not as built up and as full of people as it is today. I was expecting to 'hit the wall' at some point but must have missed it as I was having so much fun. I am sure the number of spectators cheering me on carried me along over the last few miles. Time seemed to pass so quickly and my target of four and a half hours was comfortably beaten, clocking 4:21. Oh what a day… what an event. My first… and still my favourite marathon. I managed to secure an entry into the London Marathon a few more times and always ran in fancy dress. That first marathon was so special that I wanted to experience it all again. I have pounded the streets of London dressed as Eve, a black spider, a green joggasaurus, a purple parrot and a sunflower. Every time, there was that great rapport with the crowd and other people running the marathon. Dressing up can be so much fun, especially when the crowds respond and it can be so powerful that the pain that can affect marathon runners in the later stages just doesn't seem to appear. I think there is something so very special about London and the crowds that it makes me wonder – why doesn't everybody run marathons – especially London?

******

Philip Dray – Seaford Striders

I have Asperger's syndrome – the first level of autism – but it was not diagnosed until I was at senior school. Because I had low concentration levels I found myself trailing behind the rest of the class. This led to me becoming disruptive, and after a great deal of persistence, my parents were able to arrange for me to continue my education at a special school, where I stayed until I was 17. Then I spent two years at a technical college trying hard to learn various skills, gaining a City & Guilds in mathematics. While there, I had a 'day release' work experience at a small local business. When I left college, I was offered a job there and it went well, thanks to the boss who understood my special needs and who spent 'one-to-one' time with me. Unfortunately, the business closed down and I had to look for other work. It was a terrible shock as I really felt that I was achieving something with that company. I tried so hard to find work elsewhere and even attended another further education course but employers just weren't interested. Nobody would give me a job and I felt let down by everybody. With all the spare time I had, I became bored and as a result, got into trouble with the police.

In an attempt to help me out of my situation, my brother, Antony, persuaded me to go running with him one evening. My first effort lasted just 15 minutes but I enjoyed it. I had never really been interested in sport of any kind at school but something in that short bit of jogging with Antony made me want to run again and further. I continued to enjoy running, though I wasn't fast and was very soon going out four or five times a week. I joined the Seaford Striders to improve myself and in 1991 entered my first race – the very flat Brighton 10 km. For the next two years I increased my training and entered more 10 km races, then upped the distance to 10-mile events and half marathons. I particularly enjoyed the Hastings, Paddock Wood, Tunbridge Wells and Barns Green 'halves'.

I had heard about marathons from watching the '**London**' on TV and listening to my fellow runners at the Club talking about the ones they'd done but didn't really understand what a marathon was, even though I was amassing quite a few half marathons. I was lucky to gain an entry into the 1994 **London Marathon** although I didn't receive my acceptance until early February, leaving only about ten weeks to prepare. I really enjoyed the experience and finished the race with a beaming smile in 5:20, but the time didn't matter. What was important to me was how I felt about myself. I had passed the bad time, left behind that period of my life that was best forgotten because at last I had found something to make me feel that I was achieving again. That hadn't happened since I was at primary school and excelled at French but then frustration set in when I was unable to pursue it at secondary school because of my poor written English. I have continued to run marathons, as well as other distances and particularly enjoy the **Beachy Head Marathon**, which is very near to where I live. On two occasions I have experienced the challenge of back-to-back marathons, running the **South Coast Marathon** at Gosport (now defunct) just a week after the London, and each time, I have run Gosport about 30 minutes faster, actually recording my PB – 4:37 – the second time I did the double. I suppose that means I ought to give ultra marathons a bash sometime! However, I have reached 20 marathons and aim to run many more. I am fortunate to have had the help of my parents who, for instance, in that first **London Marathon** explained the route to me over and over until I had an understanding of the landmarks that I'd come across – the Cutty Sark, Tower Bridge, the cobbles and so on. When I finish, I always look for my parents to let them know I'm OK. I am not sure why I run marathons, apart from the fact that I have nothing else in my life that I enjoy so much and I'm not sure how I manage the degree of concentration required to train for and complete such an endurance event, when concentration is something that I have always struggled with. I am proud of my achievements especially as it is such a goal for someone with autism.

******

Bill Young – Seaford Striders

It is very interesting how one's experience of running while at school can have a lasting effect on people. For many it was enough to put them off (for life) yet often, almost by accident, years later some rediscover running and become just as smitten as those who, for whatever reason, were able to retain their interest in the sport.

When I was 11 and at senior school I found sprint races much too fast for me, preferring instead the 440 yards event, the longest we were allowed to run. In 1948 the Olympics came to London but with very few televisions around, the only way we got to see anything was to go to the Princess News Theatre in Brighton. There they would show continuous news, sport and cartoons and all very affordable on limited pocket money. The children in the road where I lived decided to hold their own mini-Olympics and the 'event' that attracted my full attention was 'four times round the block'. I won it with ease and even when the London Olympics had finished and we continued to organise races round the roads (very few cars in those days), I won them too. It was then that I realised it was stamina and endurance I had, not speed. Later, when I was about fifteen I remember winning a silver medal in a 2-mile youths' road race in Amberley, West Sussex. The distances I competed in increased dramatically when I began taking part in a series of cross-country races during the winter months, organised by the various rowing clubs in Sussex and Kent, and these events were anything up to 14 miles. I continued to run on and off until 1960 but then lost touch with the sport for 24 years.

What brought me back to running was an advert in my local newspaper about a one-mile race in Preston Park, Brighton to raise funds for the Great Britain Olympic Team.

After such a long absence from running I found it very hard but finished the course feeling reasonably satisfied and eager to do more. A few weeks later I raised my sights and took part in a charity 4-mile fun run from Shoreham to Southwick, finishing it with no apparent problems. Then in October of that year I ran the Eastbourne 10-miler and shortly afterwards a friend suggested I should enter the 1985 **Seven Sisters Marathon**. The 'London' had been going for four years and running marathons was becoming the thing to do and it did seem to be a natural progression from the events I'd done. As part of my build up I ran the M25 Ten mile race, which presented me with the unique opportunity to run along a motorway before it became a race track of a different kind!

The day of the Seven Sisters arrived and little did I know what lay ahead because 14 miles was the furthest I had ever run and that was many years ago. In those days, the 'Sisters' was held in February and that year there had been a lot of snow and I began to wonder what I was doing there. The low temperatures were made worse by a strong chilly wind, making the conditions pretty grim, not the ideal setting for one's first marathon. However, I finished in 6:15 and despite the experience, or because of it, I was bitten by the marathon bug and for the next 18 months I was competing in races about twice a month, including my first **London Marathon** and the inaugural Hastings half Marathon. With all the racing I was doing I was steadily getting stronger and faster (relatively speaking) but the most significant milestone in my running was when I joined the newly-formed Seaford Striders Running Club in October 1986. Being part of a friendly enthusiastic club had a very uplifting effect on my running. Putting like-minded people together within the inspiring framework that is the running scene, enriches our sport beyond measure and adds to the potential of each runner, not least through the depth of camaraderie. When I ran the 1987 **London Marathon**, which I did to raise funds for the Royal Sussex Hospital in Brighton after a good friend, Alan Horrobin, had died in a car crash at the age of 21, I was hoping to set a PB by running under 4 hours. The day went well but it was 'touch and go' as to whether or not I would achieve my target. A group of workmates from Parker Pen Company had gathered by the turning into Northumberland Avenue (old route) and their cheers boosted me at a crucial stage (about 24 miles) when I was really starting to struggle. Then a very strange thing happened to me as I was heading towards Westminster Bridge and the finish. The crowds were massive with the noise deafening and increasing in volume, yet, I still say to this day that over all the thunderous noise, I heard a voice as clear as day saying "Come on Bill, you can do it." There was no doubt in my mind that it was the voice of my friend, Alan, in whose memory I was raising money.

Although I continued to compete at all distances from 5 km up to ultra marathons, it was marathons that really captured my interest. Perhaps it was not feeling obliged to go as fast as possible, which can easily be the case in 10 kms and 10-milers when you're trying to hold a fast pace. The marathon, however, gives you time to think, time to pace yourself through the highs and lows, and to enjoy the scenery and the camaraderie. It's almost like working through a 4, 5 or 6-course meal compared with a single plate of 10 km running. When the Striders' Club Captain, Martin Bulger reached his hundredth marathon on his fiftieth birthday and I was 63 and on my sixty-seventh marathon, he suggested I should aim to complete my hundredth on my seventieth birthday. That meant five a year, and for a while I seemed to be on course until my ninety-third at London in 2004.

Shortly afterwards, I was diagnosed with prostate cancer and some cancer cells had spread to the bones in the right leg and hip area making them weak. My consultant said "No more running or jogging again ever, for fear of damaging the bones when running or jogging on hard surfaces like tarmac or concrete." He could not confirm how many years I had to live, but if I responded to the right treatment it could be as long as 15 to 20 years. I asked him if I could walk the remaining seven marathons, to which he smiled and said "You don't give up, do you... but yes, providing you use great care. Remember your bones are weakened by the cancer. Also in view of your age, should you fracture or break any bones in your leg they will take that much longer to heal."

I started the treatment immediately. My partner, Glynis and I decided to get married and eventually began to prepare for the 2004 **Beachy Head Marathon**. When race day arrived I was obviously feeling quite nervous even though I knew the course well and had done a reasonable amount of training. Glynis was at most checkpoints making sure I was OK and not having any problems and the course seemed to be dotted with so many friends, all wishing me luck. I finished in 8:37 and importantly, with nothing more than the usual aches and pains after a marathon.

The **Steyning Stinger** in March 2005 (formerly The Chanctonbury Marathon) was next on my list (number 95). This is a very tough event and was made more difficult with overnight snow

171

and ice puddles. The day was brilliant sunshine and by late morning the melting ice and snow made for very hazardous muddy conditions... something I could have done without, fearing I could so easily slip and break something. However, I finished it unscathed, in 7:03 then set my sights on the **Rottingdean Windmill Marathon** in July of that year and number 96. There were many moments when that marathon tested my resolve to the limit, not least the climbs up Itford Hill and Mount Caburn, and the knee-trembling steep ascent up Kingston Hill at 20 miles, made worse by extreme heat, which is something that makes me struggle even on a flat course. My time of 9:34 may look horrendously slow but I knew that it was the toughest of the seven marathons that I'd set myself to walk... and as if to confirm that fact, just a week later, fully recovered, I completed number 97 when I clocked 7:06 in the **Chichester Challenge Marathon**.

There's no such thing as a soft marathon but the **Isle of Man Marathon** (August 2005) was perhaps the easiest of the events in my quest to reach my target of 100 marathons. Fittingly, my race number was 98 and despite a huge blister on my right foot that made the second lap particularly painful, I recorded 7:16. Shortly after finishing I blacked out for a few minutes and although it was probably only down to dehydration, the doctor told me not to do the other races that were programmed for the rest of the week in the Isle of Man Running Grand Prix series.

Marathon number 99 was the **Beachy Head** in October 2005 and it's my favourite off-road marathon. On the day, I was accompanied by fellow Strider, Ken Browning, and had even more encouragement than usual from other runners and spectators. Their support really lifted me and helped me to keep going to the finish. My 9:28 was the slowest I'd ever taken to do the Beachy Head but it didn't matter because deep down, I was probably half-thinking about number 100 and knew then, more than at any other time that I was going to achieve my goal.

London 2006 was just a week away from my seventieth birthday and despite prostate cancer, despite the treatment and being confined to walking instead of running and in spite of the toughness of five of the last six marathons, I was facing the last '385 yards' of my marathon running career and it was definitely going to be a special day. Walking every step of the way with me was my son Rob, his partner Sam and my stepdaughter Helen. I am so proud of them. We were surprised to be joined at the 9-mile point by Peter Graham, the Secretary of the 100 marathon Club, who walked with us to the 17-mile mark and was so supportive. We finished in 9:40 and had battled against poor weather with heavy showers at times. Also with me was my wife Glynis, her eldest daughter Toni, son-in-law Paul and grandchildren Rachel and Nathan... a real family occasion, and even though I signed off with a PW, I had achieved my ambition.

Since my diagnoses it brings home that life should never be taken for granted, and having to walk any future events, I am still hopeful that I will attain whatever goals I set myself. I will always be grateful to my GP for the last thirteen years – Dr Alan Barker. He has always given me the best advice and this also applies to my two consultants Mr Thomas and Dr Deutsch and their staff who have been absolutely marvellous. In June 2006 I was discharged from hospital as my PSA had dropped to 3.6. Interestingly, Mr Thomas said that when I first started my treatment he could not be sure how things would work out... and that my response to it was due in part to my high level of physical fitness. I don't think they fully understand why people run marathons but they have been extremely supportive towards me and they are surprised that my right leg and hip are coping with what I do, considering that they have been weakened by the cancer.

So, over the last twenty-one years, why have I spent so much time running, with the emphasis mainly on the marathon? There is no doubt it can be addictive but that may be no more than any other sport one enjoys. Initially, I suppose it is being able to say "I've run a marathon," but then you start to wonder if you could have done it quicker. So you try another one... then another and before long you find yourself getting quicker, and the total grows. Obviously, courses vary considerably and you go looking for courses that may give you a PB. After a while I realised it was not worth bothering about the time so much but more about completing some of the tougher courses. On any marathon when you find the going getting tough and you begin to struggle, you can frequently look around and notice others in the same state. Inevitably you start talking and then one or two others join in forming a small group and more often than not, it is this camaraderie that keeps runners going.

I do not intend doing any more marathons as I feel I have achieved my goal and do not want to push my good luck and health too far even though my PSA has dropped to 3.3. However, I still have other targets and still intend to compete, walking up to the half marathon distance.

I hope that any runners or walkers who read my story take some inspiration from it because it has not been just about me but more what I do, what I've done and what I've seen. I believe it's important to look forward, to be positive and, regardless of one's ability, to enjoy your running as there will always be targets to set and goals to achieve.

Chapter 9

Another Short Story

INTO THE FOG AND MISSED

I finally realised that the long and arduous car journey I'd just endured had been worth it as I drove along the short but picturesque seafront and parked close to an ice cream kiosk. Through the day the sun had followed me, caught me up and then led me enticingly to my destination: a weekend break at the Sunset Hotel in Porthgranda on the West Coast. I opened the car door and peeled myself off the seat then slowly but triumphantly stretched my way to the kiosk.

I sat on the wall that skirted the harbour, my feet dangling casually towards the sand and bit into an ice cream cone. Perhaps it was selfish of me to leave the family behind but to be honest, it had been hell at work for so long and I needed a complete break from everything and everyone. Just a long weekend away was all I wanted and the chance to switch off and unwind. I was certain that after a few days here I'd return feeling rested and ready to face life again.

That evening, after a good meal and a few drinks at the bar, I returned to my room, finished off the crossword and switched on the TV just in time to catch the local news and weather. The following morning, I had decided, was going to be for me. I was going to indulge in doing nothing in particular and being answerable to no one. The holiday season hadn't quite begun so everywhere was relaxed and manageable. Just what I wanted and I was able to stroll along the prom anonymously and unchallenged. When your job holds you prisoner for every minute of the day and you are surrounded all the time by milling throngs making constant demands on you, so that you can't switch off, an empty harbour wall, restful tide and a huge expanse of blue sky is heaven on earth.

175

The grey and yellowy brown stone walls of the shops that lined the seafront seemed to harmonise delightfully with the gentle tranquillity of the town and surrounding green and jagged hills. There was no gaudy, incongruous violence of colour and tat blaring out from the shops like in many resorts but instead, just the contented faces on the people and the natural unhurried beauty everywhere. I bought a newspaper and an OS map of the area, a few energy snack bars and some bottled water.

"You planning a walk?" asked the girl behind the counter, when she saw the local map.

"Yes," I replied, "well, no actually, not a walk but a run, a long distance run. I thought I'd head out along the coastal path north to the next village then run back via an inland route."

"Well, you be careful," she said, with strangely more than just polite customer care in her voice. "That path can be dangerous, 'specially when the mist rolls in, and it can appear so suddenly, just when you're not looking, making you easily lose all sense of time and direction."

"Thanks for the advice, young lady. I'll try not to be the chap who went out into the fog and missed then," I joked, trying to make light of her unusual warning.

After a bit of lunch I returned to the hotel to change into my running gear. I put on my favourite marathon T-shirt and a pair of bright orange shorts.

"They'll not lose me in the mist wearing these shorts," I thought to myself, then I strapped on my red and blue bum bag, containing a water bottle, sunglasses, energy bars and some money. I donned my trainers, grabbed the OS map and left the hotel.

As I walked along the seafront towards the cliff path I began to feel the sense of excitement that always invaded my thoughts at the start of a long run, and I broke into a gentle jog. Running was my pastime and my release, a thoroughly enjoyable escape from the hassles and nonsense of modern life. The enjoyment of running and the feel good factor that it creates are well known, but for me, it was more than that. It was sensing that I was in some way acting out the skills that had been handed down to me from my caveman ancestors, who could run continuously until they caught their next meal. The human body was designed to run all day but modern sedentary lifestyles were destroying this inheritance, destroying one of the reasons that put us at the top of the tree in the animal kingdom.

The sun was high and unseasonably warm, and the girl in the shop I had seen earlier was standing by the shop door as I jogged by. She waved and I waved back.

"See you in about two hours," I called out cheerfully, and feeling eager to reach the cliff path or perhaps to impress the girl, I increased my speed and headed for the turning just past the pub that would take me to the edge of the village and up the footpath towards the cliff.

Within minutes I had reached the top of the hill that overlooked the village. I paused to take in the view, and then continued on. Looking ahead I could see the path dipping and rising as it hugged the rugged, undulating cliff edge, and soon had settled into a steady pace of quiet, rhythmic running strides. My body switched on to automatic and all I had to do was steer, enjoy the scenery and the feeling of being able to run forever. After about half an hour of effortless running along the stunning coastline, I stopped for a drink and a brief check of the map.

"Another 30 minutes or so and I should be in Trebourne," I murmured to nobody and began running again.

The sun was hot on my back but the slight breeze that whispered up from the sparkling sea far below had a pleasantly cooling effect. The path was safely about five metres away from the cliff edge but still gave me a good view of the sea. Certainly, I'd have early notice of any sea mist rolling in. However, today was clear right to the horizon. Some gulls were cruising aimlessly over others that were lazily drifting around in small groups on the calm sea. I inhaled the sea air that had been cleaned by thousands of miles of ocean and it tasted intoxicatingly pure and unpolluted.

As I jogged down a particularly steep and rutted part of the path, I looked away from the hypnotic azure sea to pick my way carefully past the rocks and loose shale that briefly littered the path. They were strangely wet and slippery so I steadied my pace and began to concentrate. The air was damp too so I glanced back out to sea. It was still bright and sparkling but on looking back at the path, I became aware of a silent wave of mist crossing in front of me from inland. Surprised by its sudden appearance and its arrival from an unexpected quarter, I momentarily forgot about the state of the path just as it dipped away even steeper. It was then that my left foot slammed into a rock that was jutting out and I lurched forward like a trapeze artist lunging for the next swing and instinctively put both hands out in front of me. In that split second my mind flashed back to when I was a lad at school and, in a PE lesson, was attempting a daring gymnastic vault lengthways over a pommel horse. In mid vault, time seemed to stand still as I sailed helplessly through space before fluking a convincing forward roll on the gym mattress.

I was engulfed by the mist and hit the ground, hands, elbows, chest then knees and slid further down the grassy slope. Thankfully, I had cleared the rocky bit of the path but as I lay there, I did feel dazed and shocked, then confused.

"Was I injured?" I thought as I lay there.

I rolled over, there was no pain. I wriggled my fingers and toes then sat up. Perhaps I did feel slight pain, in my elbows but when I stood up, it was then that I realised I was trapped in the mist which was so intense that I could see absolutely nothing. I felt transfixed, rooted to the spot. I just couldn't take a single step because my brain had no information to advise my legs on even the smallest movement.

"A fat lot of good these bright orange shorts are now," I mumbled. Even I couldn't see them and I was wearing them. I stood motionless for a few moments, unsure what to do, then I opened my bum bag and took out my water bottle for a drink. I closed my eyes and tried to recall the cliff edge and to picture the direction in which I must have fallen. Determined to do something positive, I began to shuffle sideways until I sensed that I'd moved about thirty metres or so. Then, because I'd not found the cliff edge, decided that I must be moving inland and away from danger.

I moved a few steps more and the mist began to clear, and minutes later it had completely gone. I then found myself walking towards a village so I resumed my running with only slight discomfort from the tumble. The sun seemed very bright after the dullness of the mist so I put on my sunglasses to soften the glare then, while still running, checked the map to work out which village it might be that I was approaching. I stopped running and looked at the map again. It didn't make sense. Porthgranda and Trebourne were there but in between were just fields and moorland stretching back from the coast for several miles, with no sign of a village. Intrigued, I closed the map and began to run again. It looked a very small village, perhaps a dozen or fifteen closely packed houses with smoke rising from a few chimneys. I could see no one and there was not the slightest noise coming from the village, just an empty calm, and on reaching the first house I slowed to a jog, then a walk. The path became a rutted track as it passed between a row of typical moorland houses, and two ladies dressed in rather sombre-looking old-style clothes were standing talking by an open door. As I passed, I offered a friendly "good afternoon" and smiled but instead of them returning the politeness, they stared back with a fearsome scowl. Then one of them went inside the house and slammed the door while the other dashed across the track and into the house opposite. Although feeling slightly baffled by their odd reaction, I nonetheless carried on along down the lane and round the corner.

"Hello, good afternoon," I said again as I approached a small group of people but stopped abruptly as they quickly spread out across the lane forming a barrier.

"Be gone stranger, be gone," said the tallest one.

"Stranger be gone, stranger be gone," chorused the others, angrily, and they began to walk menacingly towards me.

"What was happening?" I wondered, "why are they so angry or frightened and why are they also dressed so strange?" It looked for a moment as if I had walked into a film set of some period drama and I began to back up.

"Look," I said, smiling nervously, "I've just jogged over from Porthgranda and taken a wrong turning in the mist, that's all." I kept shuffling uneasily backwards as they continued to walk aggressively towards me.

"Stranger be gone, stranger be gone," they repeated, and then one of them lobbed a stone, hitting me on the side of the head, dislodging my sunglasses. They fell to the ground but I didn't stop to pick them up. Instead, I turned and started to run back up the lane. A door opened and someone hurled a greenish liquid at me from a huge bucket then several more stones hit me, on the back of the head, left shoulder and lower back. As I sped past the last house and headed back the way I came, I could still hear them chanting "stranger be gone, stranger be gone," and more stones were thrown so I kept a fast pace hoping perversely that the mist would return and shield me from the angry villagers.

My mind was swimming, not just from the physical exertion of running fast uphill but also from trying to make sense of the last few minutes. My leg muscles were screaming out to stop and my pulse rate had gone sky high but there was something telling me not to stop.

I had once entered a 30-mile race years ago and after about sixteen miles had found myself in the lead. On that occasion, the fear of being caught seemed to override my tiredness and just made me run even faster. It wasn't until I'd actually crossed the finishing line and won the race then waited twenty minutes for the second placed runner to finish that I realised how unnecessary my fear had been.

I reached the cliff path and stopped, then very warily looked back towards the village. Thankfully there was no one there, in fact, I couldn't even see the village, just the hills and valleys of the moor stretching as far as the eye could see. I began jogging again, heading back towards the town of Porthgranda but still kept nervously looking back to see if I was being followed.

I soon reached the top of the hill that overlooked Porthgranda, where I'd paused soon after the start of my venture, and not feeling quite ready to return to civilisation I sat down for a rest. The warm sun had dried me out after the soaking I got from that green odd-smelling liquid and I glanced around me for some sort of reassurance or answers to my strange experience. The gulls were still there and the sea looked breathtakingly beautiful and I looked down at the town and could see my hotel and the ice cream kiosk on the sea front. Each piece of normality that I picked out seemed to put more and more doubts in my mind as to what I'd really just gone through. Perhaps I'd only imagined it. Perhaps when I fell, I was knocked unconscious and then dreamt the whole bizarre incident while my brain cells were confused and bruised.

"Yes, that must be it," I thought, "I'd dreamt it all, unless of course, I had miraculously travelled back in time. I mean, no one dresses like those villagers nowadays and who speaks like that? 'Push off weirdo' or 'what do you look like in those orange shorts,' yes, but 'stranger be gone', no way, no way.

I stood up, straightened my socks and attempted to rub off the grass stains from my T-shirt and shorts. I then nodded knowingly as I realised that the stains weren't from the green liquid that I thought had been thrown over me in that mysterious imaginary village but the damp grass that I'd slid on when I tripped in the mist. As for the cuts and bruises, well, they were obviously caused by the sharp bits of rock that I'd fallen onto and not from the stones that I'd dreamt had been hurled at me.

I neatened my dishevelled hair with a few quick hand movements and feeling refreshed and satisfied that I'd sorted it out in my mind, jogged slowly but confidently down to the seafront. I went into the shop to buy some postcards, where I'd bought the map earlier in the day and selected a few before taking them to the counter. The girl who had served me before was there at the till and she looked me up and down for a few moments before giving me the change. She leant forward and sniffed the air, then in a slightly trembling voice said quietly, "You saw them didn't you?"

Chapter 10

385 yards

To have a dream, an ambition, is a human condition.
To run a marathon is to live that dream.

The contributions from marathon runners in this book, each have a different story to tell, and whether theirs is a short concise account or a long and detailed one, they all reveal common factors that are perhaps clues as to why we run marathons – for the challenge, enjoyment and camaraderie for instance, but perversely, another factor is not really knowing why! The different reasons for taking up running in the first place combine to paint a colourful picture of human endeavour, mixing the most frequent response, of being inspired by something – like the **London Marathon** on TV or someone – like Jim Peters or Paula Radcliffe, with such explanations as the 'born to run' accounts in this book from Julia Armstrong and John Leather. There are the 'almost by accident' reasons, like involvement in one sport that led to a commitment to running – Kay McDonald became a runner via karate, Hugh Graham via rugby and John McFarlane from a 'keep fit' lifestyle. My energetic childhood and that of David Beattie and Jenny Mills could have been our particular prompt to becoming a marathon runner, while Jane Webster married into marathon running and Debbie Pentland's amazing battle against an illness adds yet another approach.

The marathon distance contains all that is beautiful about the sport of running but it is the last quarter, the final 6 or 7 miles that sets it apart from other events. As former world-record holder, Czech runner, Emil Zatopek once said, "If you want to run, then run a mile. If you want to experience another life, then run a marathon." Many runners will say that the marathon doesn't really start until the 20-mile mark has been passed. Even world-class athletes at the front of big city marathons will often stay together as a group until that point before beginning to compete. Other ordinary runners, from 6-minute to 15-minute milers will be reasonably confident up to 20 miles, perhaps having tested themselves over the various 20-mile races that are available around the country. Twenty is a bold, clear and decisive number which subconsciously compounds the notion that it is a barrier, so when you break through it in a marathon you are moving into territory that requires more than just physical power to see you to the finish.

At 20 miles you may momentarily visualise the remaining 10 km to the finish and picture in your mind how easy you run that particular distance on one of your regular training routes. Whether or not your legs fully appreciate the connection, part of your brain quickly assesses the situation and because it was searching for a positive input to cope with the 18-22 miles section (perceived by some as the breakpoint) it grabs the idea and with a glance at the watch, calculates a probable finishing time. I could be feeling fresh or jaded at 20 miles but I can usually predict my time quite accurately, especially if I know the course. Very rarely have I finished slower than expected. Whether I think that the last 10 km is going to take 45, 55 or even 65 minutes, I have to make allowances for the increasing excitement factor, the second (or third) wind and the sheer thrill of finishing strongly that takes over, resulting sometimes in a very much better time.

At the 25-mile point, again I try to visualise the remaining distance in ways that help – 5 laps of the track, for instance, and I think – easy, a doddle, I can manage that and find myself running faster, picking off stragglers with confident ease. Always aware that by lengthening my running pace it may not please my calves, I try to stay relaxed, running soft and light-footed, breezing over the surface and at the same time, trying to remember those amazing TV images from twenty or so years ago of Steve Cram storming down the home straight to claim a world record with such relaxed ease as to defy the speed he was actually doing.

The final push as you pass the 26-mile sign post should be the most enjoyable moment of the whole marathon because although back at 20 miles when you were hopeful of finishing, and more certain at 25, now you know that you're going to finish. This fact has the ability to override every doubt, every aching molecule of your body and fire you up to finish with a smile and a flourish.

To identify the last part of a marathon as the reason why they are different from other races does not explain why this section makes runners repeatedly tackle the marathon. Why are there thousands of runners in this country with more than twenty marathons under their belt and hundreds with over a hundred to their name? I don't believe it's because we are masochistic, compulsive or slightly mad and it is a fact that marathons are very tough, and present a physical pain barrier that should or could prevent completion of the distance. This pain can be anything from mild discomfort to excruciating terminal torture which, when added to the post-race effect of running a marathon – those moments when for instance, you have to walk down stairs backwards, decline to run for a bus or seem unable to pick up something that's dropped on the floor – ought to be sufficient to deter a normal person from doing it again. Do we therefore make a mental list of the pros and cons of running a marathon then add up the ticks and crosses and decide that the enormous cross next to the word 'pain' is clearly outweighed by the brightly-coloured, lights-flashing ticks everywhere else in the list? It can't be as simple as that, can it? After all, pain is pain. Pain is the body's way of saying "stop, this is wrong. Please avoid this situation in the future."

If we ran six marathons in one year, would we also want to have six sessions of painful dental treatment in one year, six attacks by an angry dog, six bouts of food poisoning or suffer six occasions when your football team loses 6:0. No, we wouldn't! which means that the pain endured during and after running a marathon is somehow different... and acceptable... Why??? What sort of power do those ticks on the list wield over that enormous cross. What's more, how does the message of that power pass through the atmosphere via television pictures every April to persuade new recruits to run a marathon? Why aren't they put off by the images of painful failure? Those magnificent St John Ambulance and Red Cross people aren't there to spectate!!!

Runners who arrive at the starting line of their first marathon having 'risen through the ranks' rather than those attracted by seeing the **London Marathon** on TV ought to be able to offer a better clue as to why we run marathons because they would have developed a sounder, more informed reason for running one.

From a base of track running and cross-country running, the athlete might increase his training mileage and, finding it enjoyable, increase it further. Five miles can easily become ten when it's enjoyable, and doing ten miles as your longest run can fairly easily become your 'base line' distance with thirteen or fifteen miles being your top run. This gradual increase could be likened to moving along a tunnel in expectation of the light at the end of it, and it doesn't take much in the way of wordplay to suggest that in reaching the end of the tunnel and running into the light, one reaches the point of enlightenment. As Julia Armstrong wrote in Chapter 4, "… it has been possible for me to glimpse my soul, revealing many of its facets and to see the flame that burns bright within, and to know even if for only a split second that innate talents lie within me, and potential beyond anything I ever dreamed." Could that be the explanation of what drives us to run a marathon?

Frequently, during a marathon, I've asked other runners who briefly happen to be holding the same pace as me, why they run marathons. After an initial pause to absorb this 'out of the blue' challenge from a total stranger they begin with the easy answers, like camaraderie and 'running through lovely countryside,' but then follow those with more faltering comments, ones that seem to have reached their lips from some unknown source. They'd offer "it takes you to a different part of the brain," or "you move into a different world," – comments that are answers but not explanations. Is that as annoying as the 'free beer tomorrow' sign behind a pub bar? During the 2006 **Isle of Wight Marathon** I ran the last 8 miles with a lady, called Sharon I think, who told me that the reason she began training for a marathon was as an antidote to post-natal depression.

Every time, when I think someone has found the answer, the more they say, the more the deep truth seems to melt away, leaving instead just an interesting 'why we run' or at best 'why we run a marathon' but not what it is that makes us run them again and again.

Where's Hercule Poirot when you need him...? but then, he wouldn't know the answer anyway... he wasn't a runner. What about Albert Einstein? Would he have known...? but as he once wisely said, "Imagination is greater than knowledge," so if that is true, he wouldn't know either... I should ask instead, the inventor of the chocolate frying pan, the square beef burger or the inflatable pincushion.

Of all the simple responses that try to explain why we run marathons repeatedly, probably the most powerful one, and most frequently mentioned by runners, is the camaraderie that engulfs everyone. Could it be that it's the marathons themselves that generate camaraderie or is it the type of people who are drawn to them, all bringing a similar sociable nature to the sport? Do marathons bring out the best in people...? And if so, why? There is no doubt in my mind that runners do inspire other runners. When I'm running a marathon, I am at peace with the world, which means that I am at peace with my fellow runners. I love to listen to their stories and share their humour. There's a generous spirit that flows as freely as the beer on a good night out, and it serves to enhance a runner's performance... the spirit, that is, not the beer.

I have come across the odd runner who thinks that marathons are overrated and nothing special, that because of its variety of distances before being standardised after the 1908 Olympic event, it cannot be taken seriously. Not only that, because it has become achievable by so many and for some, so easily completed and therefore not sufficiently challenging, it should be increased to 50 or 100 miles in future Olympiads. Thank goodness such cynical and wide-of-the-mark views can be absorbed with the same degree of tolerance and sympathy as that afforded to lead-balloonists in the history of flight.

Just before finishing this book I decided to do one final piece of practical research in an attempt to uncover the answer to my quest. My club, the Seaford Striders, usually takes charge of the road crossing and unofficial water station at 'High and Over' on the **Beachy Head Marathon**, at roughly the 16-mile point. I positioned an easel and flip chart where most of the runners would be pausing for a drink, and in bold letters wrote on it **Why do you run marathons?** I realised that this could also provoke some rude responses but I stood my ground, smiled and offered a few words of explanation for this intrusion into their enjoyment. Their replies were extremely interesting and not at all rude!

What they wrote, and that was hundreds of them, seemed to encapsulate the whole range of thoughts and feelings that underpin the experience of running a marathon, but did they unearth the final clue?

There were many duplicated answers, featuring for instance, just a single word – *crazy... madness... insanity... stupid... mental* and *bonkers* or as Doug Lamont of Bella Houston RR (Scotland) remarked *absence of the brain.* In a similar vein were *Cos I'm out of my mind... because I'm a stupid old man... Cos I'm old and have no sense* and *because I'm a muppet.* On the surface these seem to represent the reckless abandon mindset that keeps us going when lesser mortals might stop, have to stop... or who wouldn't start in the first place. Humour is never far away in marathon running, as I hope chapter 5 reveals... and these comments (on the run) were most certainly said with a smile.

I particularly liked the dozen or so who wrote just three words – *Mid Life Crisis,* which might, on reflection, be a collective term for most of the other comments and which, if applied to my own marathon running, covers nearly thirty years, beginning when I was (so I thought) just a youngster at 28. That seems a surprisingly elongated mid life, and one that I hope will run for a good few decades more before I join the Late Life Crisis category, whatever that is. I suppose it's the period of life when at last you realise the error, or beauty, of your ways and you either demand that someone glues your knees together or you set a world record in the V95 age category.

The physical benefits of running a marathon were perhaps uppermost in the thoughts of those runners who wrote – *To keep fit... Fit body... Keep slim... To keep my weight down...* and *To make full use of my body....* Quite a few had personal targets, like *Training for an Ironman... To challenge myself...* or *For a challenge!*

How many runners have never done a marathon to raise funds for a charity? Very few, I would guess, probably because marathon runners love life and also perhaps, as a spin-off from the feeling of camaraderie enjoyed by marathon runners – two reasons why *To help others who can't... Raising funds... To raise money for charity* appeared on the flip chart. For others it must have been focusing on an alternative to something less desirable to do with one's time that generated such comments as *To get away from my husband... Gets you away from the wife (and kids)... Avoids DIY... Otherwise my wife would have me mowing the lawn...* and *So I don't have to do the housework.* But I hasten to add that these were also all said with a smile... and were balanced out by the men who said *Because I fell in love with a marathon runner* and mutterings about *Better sex life.* If we're not passionate about marathons, it is definitely passion that drives us and is so crucial to us completing them.

Replies such as *Fun... For the enjoyment... Good for you and good fun* were plentiful, as were *I don't know... No idea... I haven't a clue... I'm not sure right now* and one that was taken a step further by Fiona of Bracknell Forest Runners when she wrote *If I knew the answer to that, I probably wouldn't.*

Because it's there and *Because they're there to be done,* echoing the mountaineer's incentive, was a frequent comment and only slightly different were the 20 responses that said *Because I can...* and *To prove I can,* topped by the man who wrote – *I can. I'm on 97, thirty-two of which have been after a triple bypass op,* which is only marginally more remarkable than Bill Young's final six marathons to reach his century.

Cos of the scenery... A good way to see the countryside... Stress release... Survival... General atmosphere... Fresh air...To get away from it all...It increases the quality of life... and *It's beautiful,* were some of the more widely known reasons recorded.

When someone wrote *Compensation for all the beer,* it seemed to spark a flurry of similar inspirations, like *Cos I'm stupid and I get a pint of beer when I finish... Pub afterwards... To run off the beer...* and *Because I occasionally get drunk and then think it's a good idea.*

Interestingly, *I feel better when I stop,* from Louise of Heathfield Road Runners, *It's great when you stop* from Graham and *Feels good afterwards,* from Tony Cowell, were replies that I wasn't expecting, not in the middle of a marathon anyway.

God knows, an answer with probably greater truth than was initially meant, summed up the feelings of many while *Love it* from

Heather Daly and *Cos I love them* from Tom of RR was joined by many other thoughts of endearment.

Difficult to categorize was Andrew of K&C A.C. who wrote *When I was at school I was told I wasn't tough enough for the school footie team.* So too, Jeanette of Portsmouth Joggers who said, *Because I like the pain...* and the man who quipped *Someone told me it was a 9-mile race. Now you're telling me that after 3 hours (of running) there's still 10 miles to go.*

I bloody love it... but ask me again at the finish offered similar sentiments to Katrina of ORR who simply wrote *Not sure yet!...* Another lady said *With 10 miles to go, I'm not sure...* while someone else yelled out *I'll tell you at the end.* More untitled offerings were *So I can think on my own... Why not!... Too old to do anything else... To surprise myself... All running together... Everyone's a winner... It was a stupid bet in the pub* and intriguingly *I'm hardcore.* Consider too, the complementary double of *Glutton for punishment* and *Cos I eat too much* – One form of gluttony to solve another, maybe! Did another runner really mean to say *– I'm an idiot. It's my first and last one.* I hope it isn't, and what about *I'm a masochist* and *It's a bad habit.*

To win a jelly baby was to recognise the bribe that I offered runners to reveal all but it had nothing to do with *To prove to my brother that I'm younger than him... I run a marathon because it's too long... Because my Dad does...* and *because I can beat my running partner Neil in a marathon but not in a 10 km.* When one runner said *Cos I've got nothing better to do today...* I'd like to translate that as saying I can think of nothing better in the whole world than to run a marathon today, next month and the month after that.

Of the two comments that I've saved until the end of what I hope wasn't too arduous a list of marathon running reasons, is one that I have never come across before – *Running one marathon for every letter in my surname before I'm 50* – signed by FRANCKSEN and pointing out the letter 'S' as to how near he was to reaching his target. I just hope that when he's completed the challenge, he'll open a telephone directory and at random pick another name or move to Llanfairpwllgwyngyllgogerychwyrndrobwllllantysiliogogogoch and begin working through his address instead. The final answer to my provocative question of **Why do you run marathons?** says the least and at the same time, the most. Anonymously someone wrote – *"Because..."*

So, is the real appeal of running marathon upon marathon down to not knowing why we do it?

It's clear that they demand the conscious skills that runners of all distances tend to develop but perhaps uniquely, marathon running also has to access the subconscious dimension of human behaviour – that deep, difficult-to-explain 'something' that appears to drive us and probably did so much to prompt the delightful mixture of mirth and serious thought in my last piece of research. So where does that leave the aim of this book...? I think I'm left with a riddle... and it is that we don't really need to know why we run marathons... because it might somehow spoil the mystery? After all, who wants to read a whodunit if you know who did it?

Answer to riddle on page 106

Hi-Tec (because it continues the alphabetical sequence of the first letters)

Post Script

I think it must be the teacher instinct in me that has caused this book to end up posing more questions than it answers, thereby generating, I hope, more discussions and even greater unity within the marathon runners' world. And when the conversations begin during your next marathon, as they invariably will, about how, where, when and tantalisingly, why we run them, spare a thought about our future. How do we open the eyes of more of the younger generation (non vets) to the amazing life-enriching experiences of running marathons. They are our future. They must take the relay baton of long distance running that will be handed on to them in order to be part of something that began millennia ago, then maintain the continuum and run marathons into the future.